MW01001142

JESUS *First*

FOR WOMEN

365
DEVOTIONS TO
START YOUR DAY

BroadStreet
PUBLISHING

BroadStreet Publishing Group, LLC.
Savage, Minnesota, USA
Broadstreetpublishing.com

Jesus First for Women
© 2022 by BroadStreet Publishing®

978-1-4245-6445-3
978-1-4245-6446-0 (eBook)

Devotional entries composed by Sara Perry.

Typesetting and design by Garborg Design Works | garborgdesign.com
Editorial services by Sarah Eral and Michelle Winger | literallyprecise.com

Printed in China.

22 23 24 25 26 27 28   7   6   5   4   3   2   1

Seek first God's kingdom
and what God wants.
Then all your other needs
will be met as well.

MATTHEW 6:33 NCV

INTRODUCTION

When do you find time to connect with God? Even if we try to be intentional about it, everyday activities and responsibilities often find a way to take priority over our time with Jesus. Prayer can happen at any time, and of course it does, but there is value in setting aside a specific time to communicate with the Lord. The notion of getting alone with God to start the day was an example set by Jesus himself! He got up before daylight to pray in a solitary place. We don't know what about or who for, we just know it was his way of connecting with the Father before doing anything else.

As you quiet yourself before him and meditate on these Scriptures, devotions, and prayers, experience the goodness of his presence and be refreshed with his perfect peace. When you prioritize Jesus above everything, other concerns fade. Hope dawns with the new day. Tender mercies fall fresh. Boundless joy springs up from a well within. And you find the strength to walk through each day with grace for others and for yourself.

JANUARY

With the loving mercy of our God,
a new day from heaven will dawn upon us.

LUKE 1:78 NCV

DO THE WORK

"Be strong and courageous, and do the work.
Don't be afraid or discouraged, for the Lord God,
my God, is with you. He will not fail you or forsake you.
He will see to it that all the work related to the
Temple of the Lord is finished."

1 Chronicles 28:20 nlt

Consistency and perseverance are important factors in our spiritual development. They set us up for steady growth, and they allow the building of our faith muscles. When we are afraid, it does not mean we should give up. When we are anxious about an outcome, it is not a reason to shrink back or abandon course.

Look to Jesus. He is with you. Be strong, take courage in him, and do what he has given you to do. He promises to be with you. He promises to never leave you. Everything you do, do it for him, and he will bless the work of your hands. Keep going, no matter what, and trust him to do what only he can.

Jesus, when I am afraid, I will trust you. I will keep moving ahead in what is already mine to do, and I will trust you to direct and redirect me. Bless the work of my hands as I offer it all as a living sacrifice to you.

QUIET TRUST

In repentance and rest is your salvation,
in quietness and trust is your strength.

ISAIAH 30:15 NIV

How often have you felt at rest in your salvation? When you take your burdens to the cross of Christ, do you leave them there? When you turn from the things you know are not benefitting you or others, do you look to the Lord for help?

Jesus is a faithful Savior and friend. May you know the deep abiding peace of his presence. May you know the quiet strength that comes with trust in his eternal love. He is for you, and he always will be. He builds you up in his love so that you can courageously and confidently live in him. Let your heart find its home in his mercy today.

Jesus, I want to dwell in the liquid love of your presence. I want to know your peace that passes all understanding. I give you my heavy burdens, and I take respite in you today. Bring relief and refreshment to my soul as I look to you.

GLORIOUS MEDITATION

On the glorious splendor of your majesty,
and on your wondrous works, I will meditate.

PSALM 145:5 NLT

When we take time to meditate on the tangible goodness of God, our hearts expand in his incredible mercy. The Lord is more glorious than our minds can comprehend at any given moment. He is larger than our little lives can contain. He is purer than the most well-intentioned act of love we have ever known.

Let's take time to meditate on his wondrous works. As we remember who he is, what he has done, and what he has promised to do, may our hearts bloom with hope. He is so very good and always worthy of our praise, our time, and our attention.

Jesus, I meditate on your glorious goodness today. I remember what you said, and I turn my thoughts to what you taught us about the Father. Fill my mind, my heart, and my very being with your ever-present love that breathes peace, joy, and hope into my expanding faith.

THANKFUL HEART

Let us be thankful, because we have a kingdom that cannot be shaken. We should worship God in a way that pleases him with respect and fear.

HEBREWS 12:28 NCV

Gratitude leads us to the throne of God. It paves the way for our waning hope to be strengthened. It leads us to an ever-expanding faith. It builds the foundation of sacred trust. When we don't know where to begin as we come to the Lord, we can always start with thanksgiving.

What do you have to be thankful for today? What are the little and big things that enrich your life? Start with a heart that is open to look for deposits of God's kindness already within reach. Then, let gratitude grow and swell until worship is a natural overflow of your heart's response.

Jesus, there are so many reasons I have to be thankful: the air I breathe, the home I dwell in, the people and animals in my life that support me. I am thankful for the fulfillment of long-awaited desires and the faithfulness of your love. For all these things and more, I worship you!

PRAISE HIM

Praise him for his mighty works;
praise his unequaled greatness!

PSALM 150:2 NLT

Can you remember a time when you were astounded by an answer to prayer? Has there ever been a moment in your life or in a loved one's life that had no earthly explanation? God is a God of miracles. He restores what was stolen, and he redeems what seems lost forever. In his earthly ministry, Jesus healed the sick, drove out tormenting spirits, and raised the dead. He still does these things today.

Jesus is alive and well. He is seated at the right hand of the Father, and he lives to intercede for you and me. He is still the God who defends the vulnerable, still the one who reaches beyond the boundaries of religion, and still the one who loves perfectly and powerfully. Let's praise him!

Lord Jesus, how could I begin to praise you for all you have done? You have had a hand in more glorious goodness than the earth's libraries could hold. You are better than I have given you credit for, and I worship you today.

ALREADY KNOWN

"Before I formed you in the womb I knew you,
before you were born I set you apart."

JEREMIAH 1:5 NIV

Have you ever felt alone in this world? Even surrounded by others, we can feel unseen. Even when we have felt known, transition tears at the threads of our lives and leaves us feeling like our worlds are being shredded. There is one who understands. There is one who sees the end from the beginning and all that lies between.

Take some time to meditate on the verse for today. Before God formed you in the womb, he knew you. Before you were born, you were set apart by him. Everything he does is done with intention and love. He imagined you and created you with affection and purpose. When you feel far from connection, know that you are intimately connected to his heart.

Jesus, thank you for the reminder that you know me best and know me fully. In your love, you created me. In your love, you pursue me. In your love, I have found acceptance and a true home that never fades or crumbles. I love you!

SUCH GOODNESS

How great is the goodness
you have stored up for those who fear you.
You lavish it on those who come to you for protection,
blessing them before the watching world.

PSALM 31:19 NLT

No matter what is going on in the world, God is unchanging in faithfulness and mercy. He lavishes his love on those who run to him. He pours out blessings on those who take refuge in him. He is a safe place to abide in the storms of life. He is full of redemption, grace, and understanding.

When we live with hearts surrendered to God's mercy, we will know the goodness of his care. There is more goodness than we can imagine! There is fullness of life, love, peace, joy, power, and grace. There is so more than we can fathom available to us through fellowship with him. Let's run to him when we are afraid. Let's come to him when we are confident. In every season of the soul, he is full of goodness.

Jesus, there is no one else like you in all the earth. No one can claim to love more than you do. I trust you with my heart, my life, and my loved ones. I trust you more than I trust myself. I trust you more than my closest friends. I trust you.

EVERY OPPORTUNITY

Take advantage of every opportunity to be a blessing
to others, especially to our brothers and sisters in the
family of faith!

GALATIANS 6:10 TPT

Every day holds a myriad of opportunities to either respond or withhold love. When we choose compassion over judgment, we look for ways to be a tangible blessing to others. A kind response, an encouraging word, a helping hand to one who is struggling: these are all ways to bless others significantly and yet easily.

There is a cost to love. It is risky to reach out in mercy when our instincts would have us self-protect in fear. Fear does not promote love. It keeps us restricted when love compels us to expand. May we take every opportunity that presents itself today to be a blessing to others, those we know and love as well as those we don't. It's worth it.

Jesus, give me grace to extend compassion and mercy to others when I would rather go about my day. Give me eyes to see where I can help. Fill my heart with your love that compels me to reach out. I want to partner with your purposes today.

GENEROSITY TO GOODNESS

Good comes to those who lend money generously
and conduct their business fairly.

PSALM 112:5 NLT

Does generosity have a place in your day-to-day life? Have you made room to practice giving to others out of the excess you already have? Though we have needs, there are likely ways we can give to others without fear of our own destitution. We don't need to cheat (a system or anyone else) in order to hoard more for ourselves. In giving, we find a greater reward: satisfaction.

Jesus taught us that those who give will receive. Those who trust the Father to provide have no need to worry, for he even takes care of the birds and the flowers. Let's find ways to be more generous than we have been. Let's look for opportunities to make giving a priority. It will even benefit us as it benefits others.

Jesus, you are the most generous leader. You have an abundance of everything we need available in your kingdom. I follow your lead and choose to be generous rather than stingy. I want to know you more as I freely give to others.

UNDER HIS BANNER

He brought me to the banqueting house,
and his banner over me was love.

SONG OF SOLOMON 2:4 ESV

Today, there is a great feast available to you in the vast kingdom of your God. Jesus has ushered you into the throne room of the Father where his abundance dwells. Through Christ, you can freely enter into the fullness of the presence of the King of kings.

When was the last time you feasted on the extravagant love of God? When did you last taste the satisfaction of his kindness toward you? Have you filled up on his glorious goodness lately? Right now, there is an open invitation to you. Come and feast under the banner of his love.

Jesus, I come to you today with an open heart that longs for an encounter with your Spirit. I want to feast on your mercy and fill up on your grace, Meet me with the overflowing radiance of your presence and love me to life again. You are my Savior.

HUMBLE FAITH

By the grace given to me I say to everyone among you not to think of himself more highly than he ought to think, but to think with sober judgment, each according to the measure of faith that God has assigned.

ROMANS 12:3 ESV

Proverbs 16:18 says, "Pride goes before destruction, and a haughty spirit before a fall." We are inclined to inflate our own character and motivations while simultaneously devaluing and doubting others'. This is pride. Pride keeps us from the flexibility that is necessary in life, and it keeps us from compassion.

May we be people who choose to humble ourselves both in our minds and in our interactions with others. This does not mean we should not be confident or that we should pretend to not be good at what we are good at. Let's be gentle with ourselves and others and build each other up in love.

Jesus, I want to follow the path of your love and not seek my own gain above others. I want to be humble as you were humble. Help me to keep right perspective of myself and others. Clothe me in compassion in all things.

GENERATIONAL STORIES

Let each generation tell its children of your mighty acts;
let them proclaim your power.

PSALM 145:4 NLT

God's mercy is not on a timetable. It is not a finite resource. It is faithful through the generations. When we look through Scripture, we find many instances of God's powerful acts of mercy on behalf of his people. When we look at the life of Jesus, there are many stories of his miraculous kindness. He is still moving in power today.

We can be encouraged in our faith by observing God's faithfulness to others. May we take time to listen to the stories of God's tangible kindness toward people of all generations. No one is too young or too old to have a testimony of God's goodness. Let's take the time to share with one another in love, encouragement, and hope.

Jesus, thank you for your faithfulness from generation to generation. I know you aren't finished working miracles of mercy in our lives today, and I long for a fresh revival of my faith. Encourage me through the testimonies of others.

WONDERFULLY COMPLEX

Thank you for making me so wonderfully complex!
Your workmanship is marvelous—how well I know it.

PSALM 139:14 NLT

You are made in the image of the Almighty God. You are wonderfully complex. You were not made to fit into small boxes that demand you look, act, or speak in a certain manner. The quirks in your personality and preferences are part of what make you, you. God is creative, and he put you together in a marvelous manner.

When you are tempted to shrink yourself to meet others' expectations, or when you feel compelled to pretend that you are someone else, may you remember that you are perfectly, wonderfully, and lovingly made. God loves who you are, and he delights in your uniqueness.

Jesus, I'm glad you delight in me and lovingly accept me as I am. At the same time, I'm grateful for your love that transforms me into your image. I can throw off the lies of the enemy that seek to confine and control me, and I can embrace who you have created me to be. Thank you!

GET UP AND PRAY

Very early in the morning, while it was still dark, Jesus got up, left the house and went off to a solitary place, where he prayed.

MARK 1:35 NIV

Jesus did not rely on his own strength to get through the day; he made it a priority to spend time with his Father before he did anything else. He was not doing it out of obligation but out of a living relationship. He came from the Father, and he knew he needed the Father's perspective to help him in all things.

We can take Jesus' example and start our days with prayer. Whatever is on our hearts, minds, and schedules is an open invitation for God's perspective, help, and power when we communicate it to him. The give and take of prayer, both laying out our hearts and taking time to listen to his response, is full of opportunities for us to grow in compassion, healing, and wisdom.

Jesus, I know I need the Father even more than you did on earth. I am grateful you are the open door to the Father. I come to you with everything weighing on my heart and mind. Give me your perspective and lift the heavy burdens from my shoulders as I share them with you. Thank you.

UNCHANGEABLE

I will not break my agreement
nor change what I have said.

PSALM 89:34 NCV

God does not go back on a single promise he makes. What he vows to do, he always follows through on. Though his timing is not our own, he never fails to make good on his word. Are there areas of your life where you have gone back on your word? We will inevitably change our minds, but let's take Jesus' advice and let our yeses be yeses. Let's not make vows we are unable to keep.

The grace of God is large enough to cover our mistakes and imperfections. He is wonderfully consistent, and he is powerful enough to take our biggest messes and make something beautiful grow out of them when we surrender to him. His mercy is large enough. We will never be perfect, but he is. He always will be.

Jesus, thank you for being consistent in all you do. You are perfect in love, and you never change your mind about me. Thank you for your consistency. I come alive in your mercy, and your faithfulness encourages my heart. Thank you for never leaving me on my own.

ABSOLUTE PEACE

Perfect, absolute peace surrounds those
whose imaginations are consumed with you;
they confidently trust in you.

ISAIAH 26:3 TPT

When was the last time you experienced the tangible peace of God as it settled your anxious thoughts? There is an invitation to you today, just as there is to everyone who looks to the Lord, to find absolute peace in the presence of the God who is with you. Turn your attention to his faithfulness. remember what he has said and what he has already done.

Let confidence in God's faithfulness be the bridge that leads you to stronger trust. He is more than able to do infinitely more than you could ever think to ask him. Let your imagination be consumed with who he is and invite his perspective to transform you own today. If you struggle to know where to begin, look at Jesus' life and words. He is so very good.

Prince of Peace, I look to you for my needs, my hope, and my rest today. I need your perfect peace to surround me and settle me. I don't want to waste energy on worries that have no foundation in your love. Pour over me with the power of your presence and soothe my anxious heart.

TAKE HEART IN HIM

Wait for the LORD;
be strong, and let your heart take courage;
wait for the LORD!

PSALM 27:14 NRSV

God does not abandon those who look to him for help. He does not leave the destitute to destruction. He does not turn away from the vulnerable. He is the God who goes to the margins and heals those whom society casts out. Look at the life of Jesus, and you will find this to be true. He does not give more favor to the educated than he does those who work menial jobs. He is the God whose passionate love is the same for all who are created in his image.

Wait for him today. Take courage in his love, for he is pursuing you with the power of his loyal mercy even now. It is within your reach; don't give up hope. Don't stop doing the good you have been working toward. Keep waiting for him even as you take the steps that you have been shown. Trust him. He will not disappoint you.

Jesus, I wait on you today. Flood me with the power of your presence and encourage my heart in your promised faithfulness. I depend on you more than any other. I will wait for you and not give up. You are my courage.

COMPASSIONATE HEARTS

Put on then, as God's chosen ones, holy and beloved, compassionate hearts, kindness, humility, meekness, and patience.

COLOSSIANS 3:12 ESV

Hardness of heart has no place in the kingdom of God. Jesus did not instruct us to love some and hate others. He taught us to love others as we love ourselves, and that includes our enemies. He showed us how to extend mercy instead of vengeance. Justice is his, and it is not our right as his heirs to judge others more harshly than we do ourselves.

Let us take Paul's instruction to heart today. Let us "put on...compassionate hearts, kindness, humility, meekness, and patience." These are fruits of the Spirit, and the Spirit is always ready to help us when we ask. Though we may naturally tend toward pride, self-protection, and rushed conclusions, the way of Christ is different. Let us follow his path of love; as we do, we will be transformed into his likeness.

Jesus, you are full of compassion, mercy, patience, joy, and honor. You are filled with peace that passes understanding. I long to reflect your lifegiving love in my own life. I choose your way over my own today. I clothe myself in your compassion, for it is my covering.

PRAYER FOR MORE

O LORD, do good to those who are good,
whose hearts are in tune with you.

PSALM 125:4 NLT

We can count on the goodness of the Lord to meet us in the land of the living as we submit our lives to him. In surrender to his kingdom ways, we serve his purposes first and foremost. He is our goodness and the prize that we run after in this life. His mercy is our portion today and forever.

Has your heart felt disconnected from the Lord? Have you felt out of touch with his overwhelming love? All it takes is a turn toward him to realize he is closer than you knew. He rushes toward you whenever you turn toward him. Make a move and watch him come close. He is your tuning fork, and he will continue to meet you, transform you, and love you to life over and over again.

Jesus, I need a fresh touch of your mercy in my life. I believe that you are with me, but my heart longs for an encouragement of your truth. Reveal yourself to me in a new way and revive my hope, courage, and strength in the living waters of your presence.

SWEET REST

In peace I will lie down and sleep,
for you alone, O LORD, will keep me safe.

PSALM 4:8 NLT

No matter what happens, we can trust the Lord to keep us secure in his love. He is our faithful foundation, our strong shield, and our refuge in times of trouble. We can know his perfect peace even in the midst of our greatest storms. Jesus knew this. He slept peacefully in the middle of a treacherous storm when he and his disciples were out to sea.

Just as Jesus slept peacefully in his storm, so can we sleep peacefully in ours. His loyal love has not left us to fend for ourselves. Fear is not our master. With the presence of his Spirit to keep, hold, and comfort us, we can lie down and sleep while trusting him to care for us.

Jesus, I want to find rest in you today. Help me let go of what I cannot control. May worry not consume my heart; may anxiety not send my thoughts looping unproductively in my mind. As I lay down my cares, flood me with your peace that passes understanding.

GOD'S WORK

God is working in you, giving you the desire
and the power to do what pleases him.

PHILIPPIANS 2:13 NLT

When we are at war within ourselves, may we turn to the
Lord for help. We have needs that may have go unmet in
important relationships in our lives. In Christ, we find these
needs fulfilled. Though our trauma responses and self-
defeating cycles of shame may have been our past, it is not
our future. We get to choose, at any and every point, what
we will do with our desires and hopes.

Is there any desire to do good for the Lord? Is there any
longing to know him? That is his work already happening
within you. He is faithful and full of grace to empower you
as you continue to yield your life to him. Keep going, keep
choosing his kingdom ways, and keep letting his love work
in your life.

*Jesus, thank you for the work you are already doing within
my heart. I long for more of your peace, power, joy, and
goodness. I want to live in the liberty of your love just as
you promised your people would, Transform me and keep
doing your good work in my life.*

EXTRAVAGANT LOVE

"This is how much God loved the world—
he gave his one and only, unique Son as a gift.
So now everyone who believes in him
will never perish but experience everlasting life."

JOHN 3:16 TPT

The living expression of love came to us in Jesus Christ, the Son of God. He is the image of God the Father in human form and given to us so we could come to the Father through him. Jesus showed us the way, and he is still revealing it to us today through his Spirit.

Jesus spoke about the Father in lavish, wonderful terms. In one parable, he spoke of a father who joyfully ran to meet his son when he returned from wandering and squandering his inheritance. The son came back completely humiliated and desperate, but the father only had love, redemption, and restoration on his mind. So does our Father with us! Let us come freely to him, no matter our state, for he is full of merciful kindness, and he receives us with open arms.

Jesus, thank you for taking the humble road of humanity to show us what the Father is truly like. I come to you today with a heart full of surrender and with nothing to offer but myself. Please, revive me and restore me in your love.

LOADED WITH LOVE

He saves my life from the grave
and loads me with love and mercy.

PSALM 103:4 NCV

As Luke 19:10 tells us, Jesus came to seek and to save the lost. He did not count his life as worth too much even though he is the Son of God. He left his glorious throne in heaven to make a way for us to come to the Father. He experienced degradation, humiliation, and defeat. He was mocked and put to death.

Thankfully, that is not the ending. He rose from the grave three days later and broke the curse of sin and death in the process. His resurrection power is our salvation; his grace is our more-than-enough portion at every point. He has loaded us with love and mercy, and he continues to do so today. Let us rejoice in him, for he is our salvation and our transformative hope.

Jesus, thank you for saving my life from the grave and for the promise of everlasting life in your glorious kingdom. Make that hope more real to me today as I continue to yield my heart to you. Load me up with your love and mercy.

RUN INTO HIS HEART

It is impossible for God to lie for we know that his promise and his vow will never change! And now we have run into his heart to hide ourselves in his faithfulness. This is where we find his strength and comfort, for he empowers us to seize what has already been established ahead of time—an unshakable hope!

HEBREWS 6:18 TPT

Whenever we have doubts of any kind, we can run into the heart of the Lord, for he is faithful. He will never stop being loyal to his promises, and he won't break a single vow he has made. Even when we are faithless, God is still faithful. He cannot change from his character. What lengths his love goes! What patience he has with us.

When we need strength and comfort, we can find it in the heart of God. He is our unshakable hope, the foundation stone of our faith that will never crack or move. The power of his love is stronger than any force of fear we will ever know. We can rest in his peace and his unmatched power.

Jesus, I'm so grateful you never change. You are as full of merciful miracles today as you have ever been. Encourage and strengthen my heart in your hope. Enliven and refresh my courage in your presence. I run into your heart today.

ENTHUSIASTIC WORK

Work with enthusiasm, as though you were
working for the Lord rather than for people.

EPHESIANS 6:7 NLT

When we do what is right—not only when others are
watching, but at all times—our lives are lined with integrity.
This is pleasing to Christ, and it follows his kingdom ways.
We should seek to always do the right thing, to do it
enthusiastically even, because it reflects the goodness and
constancy of the Lord.

When we are tempted to take shortcuts in necessary work
because we do not see the value of integrity, may we
not compromise. Everyone is tempted, but God gives us
the strength to offer all we do to him whether or not we
receive the accolades we long for from others. May we find
our strength, our drive, and our joy in doing everything for
the Lord.

*Jesus, thank you for your example of hard work. I know
rhythms of rest also belong, so I won't feel bad for taking
the breaks I need. However, I will not look for ways to get
out of the work that is mine to do. Give me strength and
joy in the process, for I know work is as holy as worship.*

HEART'S CRY

Oh, that my actions would consistently
reflect your decrees!

PSALM 119:5 NLT

In the beginning of Psalm 119, the poet explains that true happiness comes from walking in total integrity. Joy comes from keeping God's ways and seeking him with our whole hearts. When we choose the paths of the Lord, we reap the benefits of his presence. His law of love is our standard, and when we live according to it, we come alive in him.

Does your heart cry out to be more like Jesus? Are you longing to reflect his decrees in your life? As you follow him and everything he instructed, you will go from glory to glory. You will be transformed into love's image as you submit to his ways. Look to the ways of God and line up your choices with Christ today. Watch what happens in your heart in response.

Jesus, you are the cry of my heart. How I long to know you more, to become more like you, and to reflect your love in my life. Be glorified in me as I follow you on the path of your laid-down love.

LIVING FOR CHRIST

He died for everyone so that those who receive his new life will no longer live for themselves. Instead, they will live for Christ, who died and was raised for them.

2 Corinthians 5:15 nlt

We have been set free in the liberty of Christ's love to live for something larger than ourselves. His love is bigger than our lives can contain, and it continually pushes us out of our comfort zones into greater lived compassion for others. If it's not, let's consider what motivations are driving our lives.

When we live for Christ, we allow his teaching to broaden our horizons. We are led by love to reach out to others we might have stayed closed off to on our own. We look to make a difference in the lives of others and to welcome and serve those in our communities. We live with open hearts and lives rooted and established in the love of Christ.

Jesus, your love doesn't just change my life; it changes the whole world! I want to follow you when you lead me outside of myself and my comfort. Give me a heart of compassion, strength, and courage to follow you no matter what.

CHILDREN OF GOD

See what great love the Father has lavished on us, that we should be called children of God! And that is what we are! The reason the world does not know us is that it did not know him.

1 JOHN 3:1 NIV

We have no greater identity than children of God. As followers of Christ, we have been adopted into the kingdom of our heavenly Father, and we are co-heirs with Jesus. Our identities are rooted and grounded in his love, and no one can take that away from us.

Have you been living in the confident compassion of a child of God? How has your life reflected whose house you belong to? Spend time in fellowship with the Spirit and look to the Scriptures for encouragement and wisdom. Worship the Lord and find his power and encouragement being built up within you as you behold how great he is. You belong to him, and no one can take that away from you.

Jesus, I come alive in the living love of your presence. I am overwhelmed to be a child of the living God. Speak your words of truth over my identity today, and may I live with courageous compassion and confident kindness.

GOD HIMSELF

The LORD himself watches over you!
The LORD stands beside you as your protective shade.

PSALM 121:5 NLT

What challenges are you facing today? Whatever they are, however in-over-your-head you feel, know that God himself watches over you. He is your shield and your defender. He will guard and guide you along the path of this life, and he will never let you go. You are under his protective shade.

The Lord of all the universe, the Creator of this world and everything in it, is the one who fights for you. He will not let you fall out of his reach, and his loyal love will never fail you. He does not get distracted, and he never grows tired. His presence is your wrap-around shield for all your days.

Jesus, encourage me in the empowering presence of your Spirit today. Watch over me and keep me safe under the shelter of your watch. Don't let me fall away from your kindness. You are life and breath to me. Do what only you can do and bring peace, redemption, and powerful breakthrough.

ENDURING LOVE

Give thanks to the Lord, for he is good
his love endures forever.

1 Chronicles 16:34 NIV

The endless love of God has no beginning or end. There is no circumstance where we are without it. There is no situation that weakens it. The enduring love of Christ is our forever portion and strength.

Let's give thanks to the Lord for what he has done. Let's remember his kindness toward us. Wherever mercy has met us, God has deposited his love in our lives. The fruit of his Spirit is good, and it is abundant. Let's look for where it is already blooming in our lives and water the seeds of where we need to see its growth. Let's give thanks, for he is with us always in an overabundance of love.

Jesus, thank you for all you have done and are doing in my life. Thank you for what you will continue to do. I want to be rooted and grounded in your love so that the fruit my life resembles your kingdom. I depend on you.

LIVE FAITHFULLY

"Only fear the LORD and serve him faithfully
with all your heart. For consider what
great things he has done for you."

1 SAMUEL 12:24 ESV

What great things has God done for you? What
testimonies of his goodness are evident in your life? May
you remember where his kindness has transformed your
mourning to dancing and where his mercy has given you
beauty for ashes. There is an abundance of life-changing
power in the living love of God that meets you. May your
heart be encouraged by his faithfulness as you consider
what he has already done.

Let your life be a living sacrifice to the King of kings. Christ
himself is your reward, and he is worth all you could ever
give. He will continue to bring redemption to areas of loss
and restoration out of barrenness as you follow his ways.
He is so much better than any lover. He is faithful, true, and
pure. He is passionate and powerful. He is all you need and
more than you can dream of.

*Jesus, I give you the reins of my life. I want to live for your
love above every other thing. You have been so good to
me, and I trust that you will continue to be. You have my
whole heart, Lord.*

FEBRUARY

Early the next morning, while it was still dark,
Jesus woke and left the house. He went to a
lonely place, where he prayed.

MARK 1:35 NCV

FULLNESS OF HOPE

This is no empty hope, for God himself is the one who has prepared us for this wonderful destiny. And to confirm this promise, he has given us the Holy Spirit, like an engagement ring, as a guarantee.

2 CORINTHIANS 5:5 TPT

Our true hope lies in the promise of eternal life, clothed in our new bodies in Christ's kingdom. Paul says this is no empty hope. We have the Holy Spirit with us now as the guarantee of what is to come. In his faithfulness, Christ will return and claim his bride.

Even now, as we wade through the troubles and the triumphs of this life, we have much to look forward to in Christ's coming kingdom. The Holy Spirit is our constant comfort, help, and guide through the twists and turns of our journeys. He is the fullness of God and the presence of his power, and we have fellowship with him now.

Jesus, thank you for the gift of your Spirit to us. Flood me with the pure pleasure of your presence as I look to you today. I want to know you more through fellowship with the Spirit. Pour over me your peace, joy, and loving hope.

OAKS OF RIGHTEOUSNESS

Let your roots grow down into him,
and let your lives be built on him.
Then your faith will grow strong
in the truth you were taught,
and you will overflow with thankfulness.

COLOSSIANS 2:7 NLT

Do you want to grow in your faith? Do you want to overflow with thankfulness toward God? When you let your roots grow into the love of God, meditating on his Word and building your life and choices around his kingdom ways, maturation is inevitable.

Will you cultivate the life you long for by putting in the work now? Our lives are made of moments and little choices. It is not only big leaps that form our growth; it is the daily decisions toward consistency and surrender. When we build our lives upon the love of God, we will grow strong and overflow with gratitude.

Jesus, I want to bear the fruit of your kingdom in my life. I want your love, joy, peace, patience, kindness, and hope to emanate from my choices. As I build on your kingdom values, build me up in your gracious strength.

LIFEGIVING WISDOM

The excellence of knowledge is that
wisdom gives life to those who have it.

ECCLESIASTES 7:12 NKJV

The wisdom of God does not tear us down; it builds us
up. It gives life to those who take and eat its fruit. It offers
strength to those who heed its words. It releases us from
fear when we follow its ways. The wisdom of God, as
James 3:17 says, is always pure, filled with peace and love,
and is considerate and teachable. There is no prejudice or
hypocrisy in God's wise ways.

As we consider the elements of God's gracious wisdom,
let's choose his ways over our own. Then, we will bear a
beautiful harvest of righteousness in our lives. When we
pursue peace over self-righteous pride, we display God's
wisdom. This wisdom is full of mercy that reaches out and
offers more grace. It is expansive and not limiting. In light
of that, we know how to measure God's wisdom against
the world's.

*Jesus, I love how pure your wisdom is. It is lifegiving, and
it is a relief to those who live by it. Knowing how abundant
your mercy is, I choose your ways over my own. I want to
live in the liberty of your wisdom rather than my limited
understanding. Thank you.*

A RESPONSIVE HEART

"I will give them singleness of heart and put a new spirit within them. I will take away their stony, stubborn heart and give them a tender, responsive heart."

EZEKIEL 11:19 NLT

God is full of power to restore us in his love. He is the God who breathes new life into dry bones. He is the one who takes our rags and weaves them into the beautiful tapestry of his mercy. What seems barren and hopeless to us is an opportunity for God's loving redemption to bring new life out of scorched earth.

God takes our stony, stubborn hearts and gives us tender, responsive hearts instead. He puts in us a new spirit that communes openly with his Spirit. He is our Savior, our Redeemer, and our renewal. No one is too far gone for his mercy. He is able to do more than we could imagine asking him to do. May our faith rise up as we offer him our hearts today.

Jesus, you are the keeper of my heart. Where I have been cold and apathetic, give me a tender and responsive heart. Move in me and make me more like you in your compassion. I long to know you, to be known by you, and to represent you well in my life.

HE UNDERSTANDS

He understands humanity, for as a Man, our magnificent King-Priest was tempted in every way just as we are, and conquered sin.

HEBREWS 4:15 TPT

Jesus knows our limits as well as we know our own. He does not simply look at us and observe it. No, he lived a life full of the challenges we face. He was as limited by his humanity as we are, yet he showed us a better way to live. He was tempted, he was betrayed, he was beaten, and he was mocked. He knew pain, both physical and emotional, just as we do.

Whatever it is you are facing, know that Jesus knows. He understands. He's been through it. And he is with you in his Spirit to help, strengthen, and comfort you. You are fully known, fully loved, and fully accepted by him. Your struggles are not a failure; they are part of living the human experience. There is more goodness available to you through his Spirit today: more love, more freedom, more peace, and more joy.

Jesus, thank you for the reminder that you understand what it is to struggle. You were fully man even while maintaining your divinity. You know what it is like to face a difficult choice. You spent time with your Father, seeking his direction and fellowship. Today, so will I.

MY GOD

Lord, you are my God;
I will exalt you and praise your name,
for in perfect faithfulness
you have done wonderful things,
things planned long ago.

Isaiah 25:1 NIV

If the Lord is truly our God, then our lives will show it. With loving trust and humble surrender, we will live out his mercy in little and big ways. We will not seek to promote ourselves at the expense of others. We won't look for ways to demean people when we have the chance to lift them up.

May our lives, hearts, and words line up in the truth of who we are and who we serve. Let's give honor where it is due. Let's offer praise and thanks to those who have lifted our heads along the way. As we honor others, we honor ourselves. As we honor God, we put everything in its right perspective. He is faithful, and he will continue to do wonderful things in his mercy.

Jesus, you are my God, and there is no other for me. You are living love and the personification of God's mercy. You are powerful to save. You transform coal into diamonds through your presence. In the pressures of life, I look to you.

ENDURING LOVE

Love never gives up, never loses faith, is always hopeful,
and endures through every circumstance.

1 Corinthians 13:7 nlt

Reread the verse for today through the lens of God's love toward you. "Love never gives up" on you. It does not leave you or turn you away. It does not give up on who you are becoming. "Love never loses faith," for it is faithfulness embodied. It is loyal and always believes the best. "Love is always hopeful." It does not go down paths of dread. "Love endures through every circumstance you face." It is constant and overflowing in every situation.

Love is always available to you. In this enduring love, we learn to love others in the same, uninhibited way. Love is our legacy.

Jesus, you are the embodiment of love. Wash me in the purifying waters of your mercy again as I meditate on the qualities of your living love. I am yours, and I come alive in you.

FAR BETTER THAN US

"My thoughts are nothing like your thoughts,"
says the LORD.
"And my ways are far beyond
anything you could imagine."

ISAIAH 55:8 NLT

The ways of the Lord are better than we can imagine. His motivations are pure. His intentions are without fault. There is no hidden agenda in his love. His thoughts take everything into consideration; his understanding is not reduced to the limits of our humanity. Though we see in part, God sees everything as a whole. He sees what connects and what doesn't.

The wisdom of Jesus is trustworthy. Instead of depending on our own interpretation of things, let's look to the Lord for his perspective. He doesn't miss a thing. His compassion takes it all in, and he releases merciful miracles of redemption within the details we cannot comprehend. Let's trust him to do far better things than we could, and let's partner with his purposes.

Jesus, I want to live according to your wisdom and not the world's. When judgment and corruption eat away our compassion and bitterness take root, there is a pure fountain of mercy in your perspective. I choose your way, for it is lifegiving to all who follow it.

CONFIDENT ASSURANCE

"This is the confidence we have in approaching God:
that if we ask anything according to his will,
he hears us."

1 JOHN 5:14 NIV

Our confidence in eternal life is not something we dredge up from our own hearts. It is the gift of grace straight from God. When we come to the Lord, we know we have his attention, not because of how commanding or worthy we are, but because of how loved we are in Christ.

Jesus is the way, the truth, and the life. He is the door to the Father, and we enter freely through him. Let us come with confidence to the throne of grace where we receive more than we can imagine. He is full of mercy to cover our weakness, full of grace to empower us, and full of kindness to draw us near to his heart of affection. Let's pray with the confidence of dearly loved daughters, for that is what we are.

Jesus, thank you for the open invitation to the Father's presence. I am undone by the powerful love you displayed and continue to display in my life. I come with an open heart today. I know you receive me and hear all my prayers.

HEART SET

"Where your treasure is,
there your heart will be also."

LUKE 12:34 NIV

Before this statement, Jesus talked about how our heavenly Father knows our needs and will take care of those who seek his kingdom first. Where is our treasure? Where do we put the majority of our time, attention, and resources? We will find the evidence of our life's ambition there.

If you are surprised by what you find when you follow that thought, consider what your underlying values are. Consider what changes you could make to redirect where you want your treasure to be. You have agency over your choices, and the first step is discovering where your priorities are at the moment. The next step is to make changes so that consistency will lead you to where you actually want to go.

Jesus, I want my heart to be set on you, the things of your kingdom, and your love's impact in the nitty-gritty of life. Please, help me. Give me strategies to adjust where I need to in order to move in the direction I want to go. Thank you.

FIND REST

Jesus said, "Come to me, all of you who are weary
and carry heavy burdens, and I will give you rest."

MATTHEW 11:28 NLT

What a beautiful invitation Christ has given us! "Come to
me, all of you who are weary and carry heavy burdens, and
I will give you rest." Who of us has not felt wearied by the
world? Who of us has not had a heavy burden to bear?
Jesus' invitation to come to him and find rest is always
right on time.

Jesus doesn't tell us to pick ourselves up, dust ourselves
off, and tighten our bootstraps. He invites us to bring our
heaviness, our exhaustion, and our laments to him. He
takes the heaviness, offers us his lighter share, and gives us
rest in the peace of his presence. May we take him up on
his offer today.

*Jesus, thank you for not just speaking to our needs but for
meeting them. My soul finds true rest in your presence as
I lay my heavy burdens before you. I leave them there and
trust that you will help me navigate the path ahead.*

JOYFUL WISDOM

Wisdom will enter your heart,
and knowledge will fill you with joy.

PROVERBS 2:10 NLT

The knowledge of the Lord is not overly somber. Though it is full of clarifying truth, it also lightens the load of responsibility we bear. It is full of peace and joy. It brings relief to our confusion. It instructs us in unity over conflict. It is confident in mercy, and it does not back away from the power of pleasure found in God's presence.

The writer of Proverbs said that wisdom is more valuable than the world's most sought-after jewels (8:11). Nothing material that we wish for in life could match the immeasurable worth of wisdom. It is almost unfathomable. All the mansions, the elite cars, the most advanced technologies: nothing compares to how valuable wisdom is.

Jesus, I want to feast on your wisdom and feel the benefits of joy that accompany your perspective. I treasure your kingdom ways more than the ways I have been conditioned to value. You are bigger than my little space in the world. I know your ways are better. Teach me the true value of your wisdom.

WRAP-AROUND GOD

What a God you are! Your path for me has been perfect!
All your promises have proven true.
What a secure shelter for all those
who turn to hide themselves in you!
You are the wrap-around God giving grace to me.

PSALM 18:30 TPT

God is not only a shelter for all who turn to hide themselves in him, but he is also faithful to every promise he makes. He is the wrap-around God, always present and always full of grace. His Spirit surrounds us and keeps us in his perfect peace. His love reaches us in every moment and circumstance.

What do you need from God today? Do you need respite and rest? Do you need peace and assurance? Do you need courage and strength? Do you long for joy and renewed hope? It can all be found within the presence of the living God. He is with you, and he is full of loyal love for you. His grace is your plentiful portion. Fill up today.

Jesus, what a God you are! You are full of all I need for the lack I am feeling. Fill me up on the abundance of who you are. Love me to life with your wrap-around presence once again as I hide myself in you.

SPIRIT PRAYERS

The Spirit helps us with our weakness. We do not know
how to pray as we should. But the Spirit himself speaks
to God for us, even begs God for us with deep feelings
that words cannot explain.

ROMANS 8:26 NCV

Weakness is not a sign of failure. It is not a character flaw.
It is part of our human experience. When we are weak, it is
an opportunity to press into the very present Spirit of God.
He is our help, our strength, and our courage. He is our
wisdom, guide, and shield.

When we do not know how to pray, the Spirit helps us
and speaks to God on our behalf. He expresses what we
cannot. He perfectly represents our hearts and longings
before the Father, and he moves within the depths of our
souls. When we do not have the words to speak, he reads
our hearts like open books. What a wonderful gift to be so
dearly and thoroughly known!

*Jesus, thank you for your Spirit who beckons to the
depths of my soul. Thank you for the understanding
you so perfectly have of all I am, all I long for, and all I
could never name. You are wonderful, and your Spirit's
fellowship is sweet and true.*

CHOOSE GENTLENESS

A gentle answer deflects anger,
but harsh words make tempers flare.

PROVERBS 15:1 NLT

When we are faced with difficult people in situations that
provoke our defenses, may we lean into the love of God
that pursues peace instead of disunity. When we return
accusations with equally vengeful retorts, tempers flare. A
gentle answer deflects anger.

Have you ever taken the time to ground yourself in
patience before responding to someone who seems
to be looking for a fight? When we remain calm and
compassionate, seeking understanding rather than fighting
to be right, we provide an opportunity to deflect anger and
soothe those whose defenses are up. Choosing gentleness
means that we learn how to disarm our own defenses and
keep from projecting our feelings onto others. In all things,
God is our help and strength.

*Jesus, I'm so grateful for your living example of calm and
grounded love. Teach me how to detach my own worth
from what others say. Keep me from making assumptions
about what others might be thinking about me. Let me be
grounded in truth and reality and full of compassion for
others.*

HE IS WITH YOU

The LORD your God is with you;
The mighty One will save you.
He will rejoice over you.
You will rest in his love;
He will sing and be joyful about you.

ZEPHANIAH 3:17 NCV

No matter what you are facing today, take courage in the faithfulness of God. *The Lord your God is with you.* He will never leave you or forsake you. *The mighty One will save you.* The all-powerful God is your salvation and help.

He will rejoice over you. The Lord your God not only saves you, but he delights in doing it! He rejoices at the chance to show you his love in tangible ways. *You will rest in his love.* There is no greater peace than the peace of his powerful presence. He is with you even now. Lean back and find rest in the confidence of his power. *He will sing and be joyful about you.* As you rest in him, let his songs of loving delight wash over you and be your comfort and strength. Oh, how he loves you!

Jesus, thank you for the reminder of your delight. You don't just help me because you see my need. You are compelled by overwhelming love that is full of joy, I want to walk in this same kind of love and live with purpose, delight, and peace in all I do.

WISDOM'S INVITATION

Give me your heart.
May your eyes take delight in following my ways.

PROVERBS 23:26 NLT

When we give the Lord access to our hearts, offering them with humble surrender, we will find greater satisfaction in him. He does not rule with an iron fist; he is a loving father who guides us through the twists and turns of this life. We find liberty in his love, and we are able to take ownership of our decisions while heeding his advice.

Will you let your eyes take delight in the ways of God? Look to Jesus first and most often, and you will find there is more joy in his presence than in going it alone. Will you take wisdom's invitation and give Jesus your whole heart?

Jesus, thank you for your unmatched wisdom that is full of lifegiving love, peace-pursuing presence, and gracious joy. I give you access to all my heart, and I invite your wisdom to lead me in all I do. I want to walk in your ways.

SIMPLE SATISFACTION

A single day in your courts
is better than a thousand anywhere else!
I would rather be a gatekeeper in the house of my God
than live the good life in the homes of the wicked.

PSALM 84:10 NLT

Have you ever had a beautiful day that was full of joy,
laughter, connection, and deeply satisfying peace? Have
you ever had a day you wished wouldn't end? Perhaps
it was spent with loved ones, or maybe it was full of
adventuring and nature. Maybe it was a long-awaited day;
maybe it was completely unexpected.

We can know deep, abiding joy in the presence of God.
Imagine your best day and then consider that a day in the
presence of God is infinitely greater. May you know the all-
surpassing satisfaction of fellowship with God in ways you
did not expect as you submit your heart to him. He is good,
and he is full of kindness, joy, and affection toward you.

*Jesus, I have known joy in you, and I have known happiness
in my life. Your love is so pure, and it is satisfying in a way
I have not known outside of you. You never leave, you are
not upset with my failures, you do not punish me for my
weakness; I could go on. I turn my attention to you and ask
for your joy to be my strength today.*

LAY IT DOWN

"You cannot add any time to your life
by worrying about it."

MATTHEW 6:27 NCV

Worry cannot move the needle of time. Preoccupation with unknowns in the future will not gain us time; it will actually disconnect us from possibilities in the present. May we learn to lay down our overwhelming worries with the Lord and leave them there.

Live this moment, this day, this opportunity with mindfulness and intention. Let go of that which you cannot control and seize what is at your fingertips right here and now. Our lives are made in moment-to-moment choices and in the connections we make. Instead of being anxious about what may happen, let's take hold of what is ours now, and give our all to it. We can trust God with the rest.

Jesus, I give you the burden of worry I have been carrying around. I don't want to be distracted or disabled by its weight any longer. I want to live fully in this present moment and with these opportunities I have now to live, love, and connect. Thank you.

LIVING ABOVE ANXIETY

"I repeat it: Don't let worry enter your life. Live above the anxious cares about your personal needs."

LUKE 12:29 TPT

As long as we are living, we will experience challenges and trials. There's no opting out of them. This doesn't sound encouraging, but it should be. We are all in the human experience together, and Jesus himself experienced the limits of his own humanity.

Let's not let worry take over our thoughts. May it not ruin our days and waste our moments. The only time promised to us is today. It's all we have, and it's all we can pour into. That's not to say that we can't work toward the future, but we certainly can't control it. Let's trust God with what is out of our reach and do the work with what we have. There is so much available to us right now in this day we are living.

Jesus, I give you my worry about the future. I cannot control what will happen even as I build intentionally toward my dreams. I trust you with the unknowns, and I don't take for granted that today is the day I have been given. May I rejoice and be glad in it!

PURE PEACE

"Peace I leave with you; my peace I give to you. I do not give to you as the world gives. Do not let your hearts be troubled, and do not let them be afraid."

JOHN 14:27 NRSV

The peace of God is not contingent upon our performance, and it does not require perfection. God does not dole out his perfect peace with conditions. Like his love, it is freely given and resides in those whose hearts are openly his.

Jesus is the Prince of Peace, and he has not changed a bit since he spoke today's words to his disciples. His Spirit is ours, and he floods the depths of our souls with unshakable peace. When our hearts are threatened by fear, we find rest in the strength of his promised peace. His wisdom brings calm clarity to the swirling fog of confusion. We can trust him in all things.

Jesus, keep my heart calm in the pure peace of your presence. I choose to cling to your truth, and I refuse to let fear drive my choices. I will not rush ahead in haste, and I will not run away. I move with you; may your clear voice lead me.

UNFAILING KINDNESS

"I have loved you with an everlasting love;
I have drawn you with unfailing kindness."

JEREMIAH 31:3 NIV

What a beautiful God we have! His love is not fickle or fragile. It is everlasting, unfailing, and ever-expanding. There is nothing in the universe like the overwhelming mercy and kindness of our good Father. He rebuilds our cities, and he redeems our broken dreams with his restorative love. He grows bountiful, beautiful gardens from the scorched earth of our disappointment.

What area of your life needs God's redemptive love? Where has hopelessness set in? May you find the mercy of God weaving new life into your story. May you see where his kindness is already at work and be drawn to his heart once again. He is so very faithful, and he is for you.

Jesus, draw me to you with your lovingkindness today. Open my eyes to see where you are turning my mess into a garden of your glory. I won't resist your love today; it is my very source of life, breath, and meaning.

TENACIOUS FAITH

If your faith remains strong, even while surrounded
by life's difficulties, you will continue to experience
the untold blessings of God! True happiness comes as
you pass the test with faith, and receive the victorious
crown of life promised to every lover.

JAMES 1:12 TPT

What images or thoughts does the term *strong faith*
evoke in you? Do you think of giants being taken down
with pebbles or city fortresses crumbling with a shout
after a long march? Sure, these pivotal miracles and
moments of glory can easily be lumped into that category.
However, persistence is as full of faith as any mountaintop
experience.

Our faith isn't made in moments of glory. It is formed from
the endurance and tenacity of moving through hardships
and grief. It grows when we coexist with the tensions of life
and do not give up hope. It comes from asking questions
that don't have easy answers and trusting that God is
greater than our understanding. Strong faith is not being
fully convinced all the time; it is continuing to believe even
when life's difficulties don't relent.

*Jesus, even in the questions and difficulties of this life, I
choose to keep trusting you. I know there is room in your
love for all of me including all my doubts and fears. My
faith is in your faithfulness.*

GOOD SHEPHERD

He takes care of his people like a shepherd.
He gathers them like lambs in his arms
and carries them close to him.
He gently leads the mothers of the lambs.

ISAIAH 40:11 NCV

When we are weak, we don't need a leader who shouts for us to do more or to be better. We need the strength of a gentle leader who gathers us into his arms and carries us when we have no energy to do it ourselves.

Jesus is our good and gentle Shepherd. He carries us close and brings us into the safety of his embrace. He leads us to restorative waters where we can rest awhile and drink deeply of his peace. He is better than the leaders of this world, and he is more trustworthy than any powerful figure. He is full of loyal love, and he will continue to guide us into his goodness.

Jesus, thank you for the gentleness of your leadership and the kindness of your friendship. You are not like human rulers who shout orders and expect others to fall in line unquestioningly. You are full of patience, mercy, and peace. I will follow you before all others.

LIGHTEN THE LOAD

Since we are surrounded by such a huge crowd of witnesses to the life of faith, let us strip off every weight that slows us down, especially the sin that so easily trips us up. And let us run with endurance the race God has set before us.

HEBREWS 12:1 NLT

Have you ever run a far distance? If you have, you know endurance is key, and it is something that must be built. But when you are running low on energy, don't the cheers of witnessing people give you the strength to keep going? You may find a reserve of energy you didn't realize you had left.

This life is not a sprint; it is an endurance run. It requires a tremendous amount of perseverance. Where are your energy levels at today? If you find yourself running on empty, connect with the greater cloud of witnesses who are cheering you on. You have people on your side! There are encouragers all around. Find those who have run and kept the faith, and let their witness build you up and encourage you to keep going.

Jesus, I don't want to carry the weight of things that don't matter in your kingdom. I don't want to be weighed down by worries that so easily trip me. I look to you and to your people for clarity and encouragement today.

TRUSTWORTHY PROVIDER

Teach those who are rich in this world not to be proud and not to trust in their money, which is so unreliable. Their trust should be in God, who richly gives us all we need for our enjoyment.

1 TIMOTHY 6:17 NLT

No matter how much money you have in the bank, no matter how many assets you hold, there is something of higher value to trust in. Money will come and go; the value of property and holdings will fluctuate with time. The value of living a life of willing and humble surrender to the kingdom of Christ will never fade.

Whatever your circumstances today, seek first the kingdom of God. Look to him for answers to your questions. Live with an open heart and a generous work ethic. Give to those who have less than you and lend a hand to those who need help. Look for ways to serve, connect, and show compassion. Trust God with all you are, all you have, and all you cannot control.

Jesus, I trust you more than I trust the economy. I trust you more than I trust my own capabilities. I trust you more than the rising sun and the shifting of seasons. I trust you above all.

HELP EACH OTHER

By helping each other with your troubles,
you truly obey the law of Christ.

GALATIANS 6:2 NCV

Have you ever been in need and didn't know how you would get by or how that need would be met? It is an uncomfortable place to be. It is a humbling experience. Christ's law of love is extensive, and it covers the way that we treat and help each other. We are not to stay wrapped up in our own little lives and turn a blind eye to the needs of our neighbors.

Whether or not you have experienced this type of trouble, may you look for ways to carry others in their time of need. It is a simple command to love one another, but it is not passive. Let's grow in our capacity to love as we stretch ourselves outside of our comfort zones, our preferences, and our self-protection.

Jesus, I know your law of love requires movement. I don't want to stay stuck in my own little world. Help me to expand in your compassion and help shoulder another's burden in both little and big ways. I look to your example.

GROUNDED IN LOVE

That Christ may dwell in your hearts through faith,
as you are being rooted and grounded in love.

EPHESIANS 3:17 NRSV

When we are grounded in love, letting our hearts take root in the resting place of God's abiding peace, faith has a place to blossom and grow. Faith and love go hand in hand. There is no true faith in God without the power of his love at work within us. There is no true experience of his overwhelming love that does not have faith working within it.

In the love of God, there is more power at work than we can realize with our human cognition. Still, we grow in grace and wisdom at every opportunity. May we go from glory to glory and expand our understanding at every turn.

Jesus, let the roots of my heart be grounded in your love. Overwhelm my anxiety with your peace. Overcome my fears with your perfect love. I believe you are who you say you are, and I believe you are at work within me.

MARCH

"I myself will go with you,
and I will give you victory."

EXODUS 33:14 NCV

FINDING HOME

He is before all things,
and in Him all things consist.

COLOSSIANS 1:17 NKJV

In Christ, all things find their fullness. He was before all things, and everything that is originated from him. He was in the beginning when light was separated from darkness, mountains were formed, and rivers began to flow. He was there at the start of it all, and he will be there in the end.

Have you found your satisfaction in him? Have you found your home in Christ? He is the fullness of the Father fully expressed in the Spirit with us. He is our eternal portion, and he is the perfect representation of all we long for and look for. He is mercy uninterrupted, love unflinching, joy overflowing, peace personified, and justice rolling. He is everything we long for, and he is so much more than we could ever dream of.

Jesus, you are my home. You are my hope. You are my peace. You are the perfection of all I long for, and you are my forever portion. Thank you for your love that meets me in exceeding measure today through fellowship with your Spirit. Fill me up!

BLESSED TO GIVE

It is more blessed to give
than to receive.

Acts 20:35 niv

When we have been given much, we have much to give. What if we spent our lives trying to outdo each other in generosity? What if our driving value was to give others everything we have received along the way? What a different world it would be! What kindness, compassion, joy, and mercy would be on display.

What is one area of your life where you recognize the blessings you have received? Take from that well today and pass it along to someone else. Did someone buy you lunch? Treat someone today. Did someone cover a debt for you? Look for ways to do the same for others. Whatever it is, do it with joy! You get to share the generosity of your God's love with others while you do it.

Jesus, you are so generous in mercy. I want to reflect you in my life in practical ways. As I look for ways to share with others, may I be inspired to do it more and more while knowing that your compassion never runs out and your resources are endless. I am blessed when I give to others and partner with your heart.

SPIRIT REVELATION

The LORD is the one who shaped the mountains,
stirs up the winds, and reveals his thoughts to mankind.

AMOS 4:13 NLT

The same God who created the heavens and the earth, who separated the land from the sea, and who breathed life into dry bones from the dust of the earth, is the God whose Spirit lives today. He is the same powerful Creator.

This God reveals his thoughts, his wisdom, and his ways to humankind through his Spirit. We have fellowship with the King of kings because of Jesus, and his Spirit dwells within us. He makes a way where there was none, leading us through the valley of shadows with the light of his presence. He has brought us out of darkness into his glorious light, and we come alive in the light of his life.

Jesus, reveal your ways, your thoughts, your wisdom, and your lovingkindness through fellowship with your Spirit today. I long to know you more, to be filled with your everlasting peace, and to be moved by your compassion. Speak, for I am listening.

EMPOWERED BY SCRIPTURE

Every Scripture has been written by the Holy Spirit,
the breath of God. It will empower you by its
instruction and correction, giving you the strength
to take the right direction and lead you deeper
into the path of godliness.

2 TIMOTHY 3:16 TPT

Are you struggling with a decision you need to make?
Are you unsure which way to go? Look to the Lord and
spend time in his Word. He gives insight to those who are
searching, and he lights the way of those who are looking
for him.

There is a treasure trove of wisdom in the Scriptures.
The breath of God breathes life upon the words, bringing
revelation to our hearts and understanding to our minds.
Where we are set free by the liberty of his loving wisdom,
there he is at work.

*Jesus, thank you for the power of your life at work
within me. Thank you for the fellowship of your Spirit
who brings wisdom and revelation. Lead me, direct me,
and encourage me in your Word. I look to you for all the
answers I do not have.*

CELEBRATE MERCY

Celebrate with praises the God and Father of our Lord Jesus Christ, who has shown us his extravagant mercy. For his fountain of mercy has given us a new life—we are reborn to experience a living, energetic hope through the resurrection of Jesus Christ.

1 Peter 1:3 tpt

The extravagant mercy of God has brought us to Christ. It has made us alive in him, giving us the promise of new life and resurrected hopes here and now. What God touches comes to life. What he pours into becomes a well of his lifegiving love.

There is abundant mercy today to meet you wherever you are. He will fill in the cracks of your understanding. He will overflow the lack you are experiencing with the overabundance of his living love. We have been reborn in Christ to experience a living, energetic hope in the resurrection.

Jesus, thank you for the living hope I have in you. Overwhelm my senses with the pure goodness of your presence. I look to you not as a beggar but as a friend. I know your mercy is already working in my life; give me eyes to see where it meets me now.

SEEK HIM CONTINUALLY

Seek the LORD and his strength;
seek his presence continually!

1 CHRONICLES 16:11 ESV

There is an open invitation to look to the Lord at all times. No matter where we find ourselves, no matter how long or short a time it's been since we've last talked to him, there is an open door to his presence.

Whenever we think of it, let's turn our attention to him. Whenever it comes to mind, let's give him our attention. It's like working in a room with a friend; you can share your thoughts with them as they come up. He is a welcome and ready help whenever we need him. He is always listening, and he will never turn us away. Let's seek him and his presence continually, for there we will find our strength.

Jesus, I seek you today. I need you more than I can say. I know you say that you will never leave or abandon me, and I'm so grateful for that. May our communication be an ongoing, open stream of conversation today.

WHAT PLEASES GOD

This world is fading away,
along with everything that people crave.
But anyone who does what pleases God
will live forever.

1 JOHN 2:17 NLT

What do you crave in this life? We should not equate craving with sin. Craving is present when we are in lack. We crave food when we are hungry, companionship when we are lonely, water when we are thirsty, rest when we are tired, and so on.

As this world fades, cravings will also subside. In the kingdom of God, there is fullness of everything we long for. There is a feast at our Father's table. There is more than enough pure water for all who thirst. There is connection with others, and loss will no longer tear our hearts to pieces. We can live to please God here and now because all our longings are, and ultimately will be, satisfied in him.

Jesus, I want to choose your ways over my own. I don't want to live in such lack that my cravings overtake my mind. Fill me up with your love and everything I need so that I can live for you and what pleases you.

PURITY OF FAITH

These troubles come to prove that your faith is pure. This purity of faith is worth more than gold, which can be proved to be pure by fire but will ruin. But the purity of your faith will bring you praise and glory and honor when Jesus Christ is shown to you.

1 PETER 1:7 NCV

When troubles in life come (which they most assuredly do), how do you react? By buckling under their pressure and going into hiding? By ignoring your needs and over-fixating on the lives of others? The troubles of life are guaranteed, but they are not guaranteed to take us out.

May you find that when the pressure's on, you are pushed closer to the presence of God at work within you. He is near, he is powerful, and he's not going anywhere. The purity of your faith is in its authenticity and the perseverance of pressing on. Allow the Spirit to work within you to transform you as you trust in him.

Jesus, I'm grateful that you are faithful regardless of the strength of my own faith. I press on to know you more. I cling to you through the hard times, and I trust you to work your redemptive mercy throughout my life. I trust in you.

GRATEFUL IN ALL THINGS

Be thankful in all circumstances,
for this is God's will for you who belong to Christ Jesus.

1 Thessalonians 5:18 nlt

Gratitude is a practice that we can grow in. It does not come naturally to all of us. It is not toxic positivity that rejects painful realities. It makes room for the both-ands of life. Gratitude is the ability to engage with what is true here and now and what is good.

What is present in your life at this moment in time that you can be thankful for no matter the challenges you are facing? Are you grateful for the gift of life you have today? Do you have a trusted friend, a home where you are free to be yourself, or a job that provides for your needs? Do you have food on the table, clothes to cover you, and water to drink? Whatever goodness is yours now, begin to cultivate gratitude for it, and watch as you begin to see a multitude of tiny blessings.

Jesus, in all things, in all ways, in every trial and every victory, and in every challenge and every triumph, I want to give you praise. You are the overcomer of all things, and I find my ultimate hope in who you are. Thank you for breath in my lungs, blood pumping through my veins, and another day of life.

GLORIOUS INHERITANCE

We also pray that you will be strengthened with all his glorious power so you will have all the endurance and patience you need. May you be filled with joy, always thanking the Father. He has enabled you to share in the inheritance that belongs to his people.

COLOSSIANS 1:11-12 NLT

Have you ever wondered why the New Testament is so full of encouragements to endure and persevere? Have you noticed that there are many opportunities to practice patience in your own life? Life's challenges will not relent for the believer. They do not go away and leave a smooth path for all who call on the name of Jesus.

We are not promised a perfect, pain-free life. That is not the gospel. Instead, we are promised the persistent presence of the Spirit who will never leave us no matter the circumstance. We have access to the grace and strength of God that empowers us to endure, to be patient, to maintain hope, to be filled with joy, to have grateful hearts, and to pursue peace.

Jesus, thank you for your presence that fills me with strength when I am weak. I lean on your love to empower me and fill me up when I am running on empty. You are my hope, my joy, my strength, and my song.

HE IS PEACE

He himself is our peace, who has made us
both one and has broken down in his flesh
the dividing wall of hostility.

EPHESIANS 2:14 ESV

Jesus is known as the Prince of Peace. We are united to
him through the blood of his sacrifice and the power of his
resurrection life. He is our peace, and there is none greater.
He has reconciled every heart to him. He has done it!

Jesus broke down every wall of prejudice that kept us
separate and has made us one. We are unified in him. There
are no dividing walls in his kingdom. There are no separate
quarters or varying classes in his family. We are one in
the blood of Christ, and we have peace in him. Are there
people we have kept ourselves separate from because of
our preferences and prejudices? May today be the day we
enter into unifying love by refusing to separate ourselves
any longer.

*Jesus, in you we all live, move, and have our being. I know
I am no dearer to you than any other who calls on your
name. We are all beloved. I will live with an open heart of
compassion that seeks to promote your peace and tears
down dividing walls.*

BELOVED CHILD

You are no longer a slave, but God's child;
and since you are his child,
God has made you also an heir.

GALATIANS 4:7 NIV

When God called you as his own, he did not welcome you as a servant into his kingdom. He gave you his own name, adopted you into his family, and made a place for you at his table. As a child of God, you are beloved and always able to come before him. You share in the inheritance of his kingdom as all his children do.

Throw off every mentality that says you are less than or unworthy of what God offers you through his Son. He has declared you worthy. He has given you his name. You are his, and you belong to him. Imagine if your beloved child were unsure of your love and care for them. How it would grieve your heart! Don't bring grief to your Father's heart. Delight in his pleasure of who you are and who he is to you!

Jesus, I am undone at the reminder that I am a part of your family. Thank you for your love that draws us in and does not keep us on the outside. I love being yours! I love belonging to you. Increase my confidence in who you have created me to be as I lovingly live submitted to your ways.

WORD OF ENCOURAGEMENT

God is not unjust; he will not overlook your work
and the love that you showed for his sake
in serving the saints, as you still do.

HEBREWS 6:10 NRSV

Whatever you do, know that the Lord sees you. He will honor every surrender you make in his name, and he will not forget a single sacrifice. If you feel you have been overlooked by others, take heart in the fact that God sees everything you do. He does not miss even the slightest movement of love.

When we work for the accolades and praise of others, we will lose steam when we are in hidden seasons. But if we work for the honor of the Lord, doing what is right because we know it is the right thing to do, we will keep persevering in his love. Let's live for his audience above all others, for he is unchanging, and his requirements never shift.

Jesus, thank you for the reminder that you see every movement I make in love. I will keep pressing into you, into healing, and into mercy. I choose to love.

JOYOUS RESTORATION

With joy you will draw water
from the wells of salvation.

ISAIAH 12:3 NIV

The wells of salvation are pure, living waters that refresh our souls. Jesus, our Redeemer, has overcome the world and everything that limits and stifles his love. He is our joy! He is our freedom. He is our great reward. There is a deep delight that comes from fellowshipping with him. Let's dive into the depths of his goodness.

Do you need a fresh infusion of joy today? Come into his presence with thanksgiving and drink deeply of his waters that bring relief. Jesus is here now through his Spirit. He is close, and he is ready to overwhelm what overwhelms you with his living love. It is refreshing, pure, and incomparably good. Drink deep.

Jesus, fill me with joy as I meet with you today. Restore my hope as you wash over me with your living love. I want to be refreshed in your present peace, enlivened in your jubilant joy, and resurrected in your marvelous mercy.

MORNING BY MORNING

The Sovereign LORD has given me his words of wisdom,
so that I know how to comfort the weary.
Morning by morning he wakens me
and opens my understanding to his will.

ISAIAH 50:4 NLT

Every morning is a new opportunity to grow in understanding of God's wonderful wisdom. There are fresh mercies that meet us as we open our eyes to a new day. We cannot reach back into yesterday, but we can use what we learned to embrace the present moment with deeper understanding.

If you find yourself dreading the day ahead, may you lean on the present love of Jesus. His resurrection life is as much at work in your today as it has been at any time in history. His restoration power is limitless, and it meets you now. Turn to the Lord for comfort if that is what you need. Borrow his hope as you lean on him.

Jesus, you know what I need before I even know to ask. I trust that you knew what was coming before I did. Comfort me, strengthen me, and lead me with your wisdom. Renew my trust in you every morning.

POWERFUL AND EFFECTIVE

Confess your sins to each other and pray for each other so that you may be healed. The prayer of a righteous person is powerful and effective.

JAMES 5:16 NIV

Have you known the power of praying with others? Have you been encouraged when someone took the time to pray over you? Have you felt your heart soften with compassion when you prayed for another? Prayer is a gift to each of us, and it is a gift to the body of believers.

Do you have a worry that just won't let up? Ask a trusted friend to pray for you. Is there someone close to you who is struggling? Offer to pray for them if they are open to it. It can be an extremely cathartic experience to pray with others, and it is, as James says, for our healing.

Jesus, thank you for the open line of communication I have through prayer. I will not only pray for myself and my own little life but also for others. Give me greater scope of your compassion and supernatural power as I engage in communal prayer.

ONCE AGAIN

He will once again fill your mouth with laughter
and your lips with shouts of joy.

JOB 8:21 NLT

Job knew a lot of loss in his life. Perhaps you have too.
There is no quick fix to easing a person's grief. There is no
easy way out of the pain of loss. It has to be lived, moved
through, and felt. Still, grief is not a singular experience.
It can coincide with joy. There can still be satisfaction and
movement in other areas of life even as we grieve heavy
losses. One does not negate the other. Laughter and joy do
not dismiss the pain, but they can briefly lighten the load.

If you find yourself in a time when pleasure and joy seem
distant, know that there is more beauty to be found in your
life. There will be things that make you laugh until you cry,
and your heart will swell with delight again. They will come,
and when they do, let them in.

*Jesus, thank you for the promise of renewed joy, of
sunrises and sunsets, of simple delights and deep
connections. Today, remind me that life will not always
be heavy.*

WHAT A SAVIOR

The Word became human and made his home among us.
He was full of unfailing love and faithfulness. And we have
seen his glory, the glory of the Father's one and only Son.

JOHN 1:14 NLT

Jesus took on flesh and made his home among us. The
King of kings, the Son of God, the Creator, became human
and lived the human experience to show us a better way.
He was full of loyal love and forever faithfulness. He still is.

Jesus did not come to show us how baseless and awful we
are; he came to show us a better way to live. He made a
way for us to be fully connected to the Father through his
Spirit and live as breathing, walking reflections of his love
in this life. He is our Savior, the one who took every blame
and shame upon himself and liberated us in his love. Let's
live as the free people we are.

*Jesus, thank you for the sacrifice you made so that we can
know you in spirit and in truth. Thank you for the freedom
I have in your love. With the mercy of your powerful
presence, touch the areas of my life that feel impossible
to face.*

PUT YOUR HOPE IN HIM

The LORD is good to those whose hope is in him,
to the one who seeks him.

LAMENTATIONS 3:25 NIV

Where our hope is, our lives will follow. If our true hope is
in the Lord, then we will live in alignment with his kingdom
values. We will heed his Word and follow his pathway of
love. We will choose to do what he has said because we
trust that he is greater than we are and his understanding
fuller than our own.

Let's put our hope in him with all our lives. Where we have
been depending on our own capabilities to get us through,
or even counting on him as our last resort, let's reorder
things. Let's live as those who believe that Jesus is who
he said he was, that he still lives, and that he will rule and
reign over all.

*Jesus, I put my whole hope in you. Not just the little hopes
but my whole life. It's all riding on you, Lord. May my life
reflect your mercy. Give me vision, wisdom, and strength
to keep living for you.*

THE SAME MEASURE

"Do not judge others,
and you will not be judged.
Do not condemn others,
or it will all come back against you.
Forgive others, and you will be forgiven."

Luke 6:37 NLT

Jesus' words are as relevant today as they ever have been. His law of love is the way of his kingdom, and there is no higher law. Where we are quick to judge, Jesus is quick to extend mercy. Where we are swift to condemn, Jesus offers compassion and understanding.

There is power in extending grace, mercy, and love instead of withholding them in the name of righteous indignation. Jesus, the Son of God, did not rule with force or retaliation. Neither should we. As we forgive, so we will be forgiven. Everything we do will be reflected back to us, so let's live with love as our highest motto.

Jesus, your ways are better than my ways, and your thoughts are purer than my own. You see what I cannot, and you consider what I don't perceive. Give me grace to extend mercy, kindness, and grace instead of judgment. I want to reflect your love in my life.

SHINE YOUR LIGHT

"Let your light shine before others, that they may see your good deeds and glorify your Father in heaven."

MATTHEW 5:16 NIV

What does it look like to let your light shine before others as Jesus encouraged? When we allow the presence of God to move within us and strengthen us as we do the work we've been given, the light of God's goodness within us shines for others to see.

Integrity, honesty, joy, peace, patience: all the indicators of God's kingdom are at work in this world. Do we value them enough to emulate them in our lives? Instead of looking for ways to hide, let's look for ways to build meaning into all we do. Love is a great driving force. In fact, it's the greatest. May everything we do reflect the love of Christ at work in us.

Jesus, your light of life shines on me, and I am free to walk in your ways. Thank you! May my life reflect your radiant glory. I love you more than I can express, and I want to show that.

OPEN HEART

"For those who listen with open hearts will receive more revelation. But those who don't listen with open hearts will lose what little they think they have!"

MARK 4:25 TPT

In order to listen with an open heart, we need to shelve our fixes and defenses. We need to lay down our self-protective armor and pride. We need to allow another reality besides our own to exist and have meaning.

Those who know how to listen well experience a greater depth of connection with others. They learn empathy, which is a deep form of understanding and care, and that will enlarge their capacity to grow in wisdom. Every day, wisdom offers us the ability and wonderful invitation to listen with an open heart.

Jesus, I lay down my foolish pride and everything I think I know in favor of growing in your wisdom and truth. I know your love is expansive and so is your wisdom. It is simple yet complex and full of lifegiving fruit. I yield to you. I choose to listen to you and others, and I trust your Spirit to guide me.

HUMBLE LOVE

Don't be selfish; don't try to impress others.
Be humble, thinking of others as better than yourselves.

PHILIPPIANS 2:3 NLT

When we line our hearts with humility, it affects how we view others. Humility quiets the voice of pride that says that we are more important than others. Pride promotes self-protection, and it keeps us defensive and pushes others away. It also over-inflates the value of other people's opinions of us.

Humility keeps things in perspective. We can be confident in our inherent worth, and we can also see the worth in others and their perspectives. It makes space for compassion, and it allows for connection with others in practical ways. While pride is like an ivory tower, isolating and disconnecting us from others, humility keeps us at the communal table where we can break bread with others.

Jesus, you practiced perfect humility in your life and ministry. I want to follow your lead. Where pride has put my own preferences and ideals on a pedestal, I humble myself in your loving wisdom.

SLEEP PEACEFULLY

When you lie down, you will not be afraid;
when you lie down, your sleep will be sweet.

PROVERBS 3:24 NIV

When was the last time that you slept peacefully? There are certainly times in our lives where sleep does not come as easily as others. Perhaps it's in the trenches of parenthood, the transitions of major life changes, or another disruption.

The wisdom of God can be trusted, not only in the day-to-day working out of our plans and lives, but also in the peace-keeping power of our rest. We need not be overtaken by fear when the wise Creator is guiding us through the twists and turns of this life. Let's trust Jesus to take care of all we cannot foresee, and let's rest in his presence.

Jesus, I trust you to take care of the things I cannot anticipate in life. I know you are wisdom incarnate. You are my loving leader, and you are my shield and refuge. Take care of me and fill me with the peace of your presence. May I rest well and be revived in your love.

LED BY THE LORD

May the Lord lead your hearts into a full understanding
and expression of the love of God and the patient
endurance that comes from Christ.

2 THESSALONIANS 3:5 NLT

When the Lord leads our hearts, he gives us greater
understanding of his wisdom. He also increases our
awareness of how his mercy works in our lives. There is
more than enough grace and strength for every challenge
that crops up. There is loyal love to keep our hearts at rest
and to set our minds at ease.

Instead of rushing ahead into our own ideas, let's give
ourselves space to consider them with the Lord. In his
presence, all is made clear. Though haste is a learned
response, taking the time to slow down and think over our
actions and plans can also be acquired with intention. May
the Lord lead us as we give him our attention today.

*Jesus, before I go off into my day, I give you space to
speak to me. Lead me in your wisdom as I make decisions
throughout my day. Speak to me and redirect me when
necessary. You are my loving leader, and I follow you.*

SHIELD AND STRENGTH

God is my shield,
saving those whose hearts are true and right.

PSALM 7:10 NLT

The psalms describe God as a protective force for those who hide themselves in him. Over and over, we see the imagery crop up. He is described as a fortress, a strong shelter, and a place of refuge. To this day, he is a safe place to run to.

When we are afraid, may we turn to hide ourselves in him. When we are unsure what steps to take, let us look to his wisdom to guide us. We are children of the living God, and he will not leave us to defend ourselves. He is our Father, and he will take care of us. Let's not hesitate to hide ourselves in his presence whenever we need shelter. He is good, and he will always provide for our needs.

Jesus, you are my strength and my shield. You save me from the fiery darts of the enemy, and you set my feet on the solid ground of your salvation. I am alive in you, and I am at rest in your perfect peace.

PURSUING LIFE

Whoever pursues righteousness and love
finds life, prosperity and honor.

PROVERBS 21:21 NIV

What would it look like to pursue righteousness and love in your day-to-day life? Would you need to reprioritize your values? Would you need to shift your perspective and efforts? Or is it already a part of the core values that drive what you are doing?

Know this: whoever pursues what is right, good, true, and loving finds life, satisfaction, and honor. As you seek after the kingdom of God, which is full of these traits, all you are longing for will be also given to you. Let's take Jesus at his word and seek first his kingdom and his righteousness, knowing that when we do, all these things will be given to you as well (Matthew 6:33).

Jesus, I seek your kingdom first and press into your righteousness and love. I know that when I prioritize you and your kingdom, I don't need to worry about the details. You are a master of details. I trust you, and I choose you.

HE LIGHTS THE WAY

Lord, you give light to my lamp.
My God brightens the darkness around me.

PSALM 18:28 NCV

No matter how dark the circumstances you walk through, the Lord is a light to those in need. He has not left you, and he will not abandon you in your situation. He will brighten the darkness around you and show you where to step and what to avoid.

Do you trust that the Lord will continue to comfort, guide, and strengthen you? Whether or not you have experienced his tangible help before, he promises to be with you. Lean into his loyal love that is with you even in this moment. He is never far away. He will give light to your lamp and lead you along pathways of his peace.

Jesus, you are the light of the world, and I am found in you. The light of your life in mine is like the moon reflecting the sun's radiance. Shine on me, and I will live. Light the way, and I will follow your lead.

NO MORE VEIL

We can all draw close to him with the veil removed from
our faces. And with no veil we all become like mirrors
who brightly reflect the glory of the Lord Jesus. We are
being transfigured into his very image as we move from
one brighter level of glory to another.

2 CORINTHIANS 3:18 TPT

In the great expanse of the kingdom, there is freedom to
live, move, and have our being. This is not reserved for
some far-off day; it is available here and now right in the
thick of things. When Jesus died on the cross, the veil in
the temple that separated the presence of God from the
people was torn. There is no more barrier between God
and his people.

Through Jesus, we have been liberated and welcomed into
the host of God's presence. There is nothing that keeps us
separate from his love, and nothing ever will. May we be
transformed by his living presence and become more like
him in steadfast love. We are moving from glory to glory in
his presence.

*Jesus, thank you for removing every barrier between
humanity and the Father. I come to you with the
confidence and humility of a loved one. I cannot stay
away! Fill me up, change me, and refine me with your
overwhelming love.*

LIMITLESS MERCY

You, O Lord, your mercy-seat love is limitless,
reaching higher than the highest heavens.
Your great faithfulness is so infinite,
stretching over the whole earth.

PSALM 36:5 TPT

There is no limit to God's love. There is no ceiling to break through, for he is boundless in mercy. Where we have felt the boundaries of our own compassion, there is an invitation to press into the abounding kindness of God's heart. When we fill up on his pure love, we have more to offer others.

Instead of going through this day trying to subsist on the breadcrumbs of our own capacity, let's spend time in the generous presence of our God. When we lean on him, he renews our strength, replenishes our peace, and mediates our troubles. His faithfulness is unfailing, so let's trust him to do what we cannot do on our own. He is loyal to the end, and he is forever good.

Jesus, there is no one else in this world who loves me the way you do. Your pure motives and unbiased affection fill and fuel me. Please, fill me up right now. Rain down on me the refreshing waters of your presence.

BEAUTIFUL HOPE

"He will wipe every tear from their eyes,
and there will be no more death
or sorrow or crying or pain.
All these things are gone forever."

REVELATION 21:4 NLT

When Christ comes again, he will make every wrong thing right. He will settle every troubled heart. Justice will shine like the sun. He will erase the loss we endure now, and he will wipe away every tear from our eyes.

What a glorious hope to look forward to: an age where there is no more death, sorrow, crying, or pain. When these are gone forever, we will be left with unending joy, persistent peace, and lavish love that is never interrupted by confusion or doubt. We will see clearly what we can only catch glimpses of now. May we find encouragement and hope in the promise of better things to come. He is faithful, and he won't stop until every promise he has made is fulfilled.

Jesus, thank you for the hope I have in you. I can't wait for the day when loss is no longer a part of my experience. Oh, that pain would be but a memory now! Even so, I find hope in your Word and in your presence.

APRIL

"Don't be afraid.
Just stand still
and watch the Lord
rescue you today."

Exodus 14:13 NLT

TELL ME

Tell me in the morning about your love,
because I trust you.
Show me what I should do,
because my prayers go up to you.

PSALM 143:8 NCV

What would your life look like if you took the time to
look for God's guidance in all things? Every day is a fresh
opportunity to experience his mercy in new, unfolding
ways. He is always at work in his powerful love restoring,
redeeming, and bringing beauty into the world.

Let's take this opportunity to seek his heart. *Tell me in
the morning about your love because I trust you.* When
we put our trust in God, we do not need to hold back our
requests for more of him. He does not turn away our pleas
to experience his love afresh. *Show me what I should do
because my prayers go up to you.* Let's never stop looking
to his wise leadership in our lives and praying unceasingly
in all things.

*Jesus, reveal yourself to me in new ways today as I look to
you. Refresh my heart's hope in your presence and expand
my understanding of your living love. I look to you, and I
trust you.*

UNQUENCHABLE LOVE

Many waters cannot quench love;
rivers cannot sweep it away.
If one were to give all the wealth of one's house for love,
it would be utterly scorned.

SONG OF SOLOMON 8:7 NIV

The love of God is greater than any passion we have felt or been pursued by in human relationships. Love is a gift, no matter the source, but the love of God is limitless. Jesus was and is love incarnate. He is the embodiment of everything God is, and God is love.

Floods and overflowing rivers cannot remove God's love. Drought or famine can't deplete it. It is more costly than our idea of wealth. It is more valuable than gold. Though we could attempt to exhaust God of his merciful kindness, he can never be emptied. It is who he is, and he is a limitless source. May we be overwhelmed by the generosity of his love as often as we turn our attention to him. He is so very good.

Jesus, I am grateful that love is not a commodity to be bought or sold. It is not a tool of control to be metered out or withheld. It is an extension of your very being, and I am caught in the depths of it at all times.

TRUSTWORTHY ONE

It is better to take refuge in the LORD
than to trust in people.

PSALM 118:8 NLT

Have you ever had someone in your life whom you did not need to wonder or worry about whether they would show up when you needed it? They were there through it all, no matter what came. However, even when we give our best, we will fail others. Even when their intentions are well-placed, others will fail us.

Though we may have faithful friends, caring parents, and consistent lovers, Jesus outshines them all. There is none perfect besides God. He is the only one who will never fail us. Let's make sure our highest trust is where it belongs in the Lord. It is a beautiful gift to have trustworthy people in our lives, but no one can be all things to all people. Where our humanity limits us, Jesus is inexhaustible. What good news!

Jesus, thank you for the perspective check today. I'm grateful for those in my life who are faithful and true friends. I'm even more grateful for your perfect love that meets me, keeps me, and upholds me through all things.

HARD WORK PAYS OFF

All hard work brings a profit,
but mere talk leads only to poverty.

PROVERBS 14:23 NIV

May we never forget the importance of follow-through in our lives. Though we may talk a good talk, talk is cheap if there is nothing to back it up. May we be people of our word by doing what we said we would do and following through on our commitments.

Have you ever talked about wanting to change something in your life, but you got stuck? It's pretty safe to say we all have areas we want to improve. If you find yourself talking about a goal more than you are planning and putting in consistent effort toward it, take some time to reevaluate your priorities. *All hard work brings a profit.* Every consistent effort is rewarded.

Jesus, I don't want to be someone who is known for talking about problems more than working on them. I don't want to be a dreamer who does not make movements toward their desires. Help me follow through with hard work and consistency. I know it will pay off in the end.

FOCUS ON TODAY

"Don't worry about tomorrow,
because tomorrow will have its own worries.
Each day has enough trouble of its own."

MATTHEW 6:34 NCV

Worry is a trap that gets us stuck in future unknowns. If we're not careful, we will spend our mental and emotional energy trying to fix problems that aren't within our grasp. Worrying is not the same as planning; worry sends us spinning while planning has a focus. Let's learn to take each day as it comes and handle the challenges that crop up.

It's useless to try to mitigate unknowns before they happen. Today will be filled with opportunities to take hold of the present moment, choose to be present with those we love, and put in the consistent work of day-to-day life. May we meet each moment with joy, peace, presence, and prayer. Let's lean into the present grace of God that empowers us.

Jesus, I give you my worries about the unknown, and I lay hold of what is within my grasp to do today. I won't get caught up in the swirl of fear when you are my center and my firm foundation. Give me vision and clarity as I lean on you to meet every challenge and trial as it comes.

THERE IS ROOM

"There are many rooms in my Father's house;
I would not tell you this if it were not true.
I am going there to prepare a place for you."

JOHN 14:2 NCV

Have you ever felt left out? Perhaps there are friends that you just can't seem to stay connected to because of your different life paces. Perhaps you were excluded from an invitation you were sure would include you. Whatever the cause of rejection, may you know that God will never leave you out or forget you.

There are many rooms in the Father's house. There is ample space in his kingdom for all who come to him. You are not an afterthought to God. You were wonderfully and intentionally created in his image. You are his, and you belong to him. He is preparing your specific place even now. You have fellowship with his well-known love through his Spirit today. Look to him.

Jesus, thank you for seeing me, knowing me, and choosing me. I find my identity rooted and established in your loyal love. You will never let me go. I'm leaning into you; refresh my heart, renew my spirit, and remind me who I am in you.

WITHOUT CRITICISM

If any of you needs wisdom, you should ask God for it.
He is generous to everyone and will give you wisdom
without criticizing you.

JAMES 1:5 NCV

Whatever it is you need today, you can find it, without
criticism, in the Lord. He will not demean you for your
need, and he will not turn you away or make light of your
request. He gives out of the generosity of his kingdom
to all who seek him. His love does not make fun of or
disparage anyone.

He is infinite in wisdom and freely gives help to those who
look to him. Ask God for what you need. Do not despair; he
won't ignore your cry. He's not too busy with supposedly
more important matters. What is important to you is
important to him. That's how love works! Trust his wisdom
especially when it challenges you. Everything he does is
done in love, and he has a perfectly clear perspective of all
components. He sees the big picture, and he knows how
each detail plays a part.

*Jesus, thank you for the wisdom of your Word. I come
to you with my questions and my challenges. I trust your
wisdom more than my own understanding. Help me, Lord!*

FELLOWSHIP AS A PRIORITY

Let us not neglect our meeting together, as some people do, but encourage one another, especially now that the day of his return is drawing near.

HEBREWS 10:25 NLT

There are so many benefits to community. We were made to live together, lift each other up in our weaknesses, and encourage one another in our discouragements. One person's strength is a strength to all. One person's pain is also felt by all.

Instead of isolating ourselves, especially in hard times, let's lean into the fellowship of trusted friends, family, and believers. We can only encourage ourselves so much; the encouragement that comes from a shared load is a balm to the soul. Look for ways to prioritize connection with those who encourage you to keep living like Jesus.

Jesus, thank you for your body of believers. I've experienced encouragement in community, and I have also experienced disappointment. May I not give up fellowshipping with those who keep sharpening me in love, justice, and mercy.

THANKFUL IN ALL THINGS

Give thanks for everything to God the Father
in the name of our Lord Jesus Christ.

EPHESIANS 5:20 NLT

When was the last time you specifically gave thanks for
the people in your life? Let's break down "everything" into
"everyone." Think through the people in your life who have
had an impact on your growth. As you spend time in the
presence of God, thank him for them.

If you want to take this a step further today, go through
every interaction with the intention of giving thanks for
each person. When you are at the grocery store, give
thanks in your heart for the cashier. When you are on a
work call, cultivate gratitude within for the person speaking
with you. Try it out today. As you reflect on it later, write
down how it affected your view of others.

*Jesus, I want to follow your loving lead in my interactions
with people no matter who they are. You always
treated those around you with respect and honor. As
I intentionally give thanks for everyone, I come across
today, enlarge my capacity for compassion. Help me to
see people the way you do.*

SOFTENED BY WISDOM

How wonderful to be wise,
to analyze and interpret things.
Wisdom lights up a person's face,
softening its harshness.

ECCLESIASTES 8:1 NLT

The light of wisdom breaks open our understanding and increases our comprehension of what God is like. What a wonderful gift it is! When we look for wisdom rather than confirmation bias of our opinions, we humbly open ourselves to growing in God's ways.

When we look under the surface of others' actions, we find a history of conditioning. This is true of us as well. May we be seekers of the truth and revealers of true wisdom who strip away the self-protective armor that keeps us stuck in limited understanding. Let's trust that God's wisdom is always expanding our capacity to love. The fruit of his wisdom is our growth.

Jesus, thank you for your unmatched wisdom. I won't overlook your sermon on the mount, and I won't ignore the words you spoke. I eat them up like the hungry soul I am. Thank you for your wisdom that softens my defenses and challenges my preconceived notions.

LEAVE ROOM

Make allowance for each other's faults, and forgive anyone who offends you. Remember, the Lord forgave you, so you must forgive others.

COLOSSIANS 3:13 NLT

It is human to err. It is natural for us to make mistakes. Even those with the best intentions will fail others. We all have blind spots and flaws. Let's not forget that we are flawed as much as anyone else. We can make space for other's faults by remembering that we are far from perfect. Accountability has its place, but so does mercy.

Petty offenses can build walls of bitterness if we're not careful. Let's remember how consistently and fully the Lord loves us and forgives our faults. Let's choose to forgive those who hurt us unintentionally. Let's forgive those who hurt us, period. Forgiveness does not mean unmetered access to our lives; it means we let them off the hook of owing us anything. Let's follow the Lord's lead and forgive others. We will free ourselves in the process.

Jesus, I know that only you are perfect. I am grateful for the mercy I've been shown over and over again. Instead of letting unforgiveness build in me, I want to leave room for others' humanity. Help me to forgive and let go. I trust you.

TIMELY REMINDER

I remind you to fan into flame the gift of God,
which is in you through the laying on of my hands.
For the Spirit God gave us does not make us timid,
but gives us power, love and self-discipline.

2 TIMOTHY 1:6-7 NIV

Today, remember what it was like when you first surrendered to the Lord. Think back on those early days of your salvation. What were the joys, relief, and focus of your days? Were there gifts that you knew that God had given you that you have now neglected in some way?

Don't use this exercise to shame yourself. We all drift and forget what was once important to us. In looking back, perhaps you will realize that even more important values drive your life now. Whatever the case may be, fan the flame inside of you. Be bold in your purpose and in your generosity. Make choices that prioritize this for the glory of God.

Jesus, it is my heart's posture that matters most to you and not what I do with my skills. I want to live a life of courageous, bold love. And I also want to unashamedly hone the gifts and talents I have. I choose to keep consistently showing up. Be glorified in my life as I do.

NO COMPARISON

This slight momentary affliction is preparing us for an eternal weight of glory beyond all measure.

2 CORINTHIANS 4:17 NRSV

When we're treading water in an ocean of difficulty, it can be challenging to remember that this moment in time will pass. Though we cannot avoid the distress that comes from living in a turbulent world, we will get through with the grace and strength of God's presence carrying us. He is our lifeboat, the wind in our sails, and the most skilled captain imaginable.

Whatever you are facing today, keep going. Keep leaning on the everlasting hope of Jesus with you. Pray and ask for renewed hope. Ask for vision to catch a glimpse of the eternal weight of glory that is being prepared. There are far better things ahead than anything you leave behind.

Jesus, thank you for your promised presence with me in all things. Your Spirit is my guide, my help, and my strength. I lean on you. I depend on you to get me through life's challenges, not unscathed, but growing in grace, love, and joy. Thank you.

LET HIM HONOR YOU

Humble yourselves under the mighty power of God, and at the right time he will lift you up in honor.

1 PETER 5:6 NLT

Jesus stated that the one who wants to be first in the kingdom of God should become a servant to all (Mark 9:35). Jesus exemplified this in his life, ministry, death, and resurrection. He became a servant to all humankind and humbly offered compassion to people from every level of society. He did not play favorites, nor did he exclude anyone based on their social standing.

Let's take the example of Christ, as well as the admonition of Peter, and humble ourselves under God's mighty power. When we serve others humbly, not thinking ourselves too good for anything or anyone, we practice the laid-down love of Jesus. We need not worry about distinguishing ourselves when we live with integrity, honor, and mercy. God will do it at just the right time.

Jesus, you are the humble King, and I want to live as a reflection of your all-encompassing, merciful kindness. I will not pull away from tasks or people that challenge my biases. I will press in with love and humility just as you would do.

EVEN WHEN

When I am afraid,
I will put my trust in you.

PSALM 56:3 NLT

Fear is not an extraneous part of life. We are created with built-in responses to threats. It is a matter of when, not if, fear will come knocking on the doors of our lives. What will we do with it when it does? One of the most often repeated phrases from God to his people throughout Scripture is, "Do not be afraid." It's in the Bible 365 times!

Why would God tell us not to give into fear more than any other command unless we are presented with a myriad of opportunities to do so? Jesus also said it many times when he was encouraging his friends. Instead of yielding to fear when it rises within us, let's take each opportunity to push through it and instead surrender to the empowering grace of God to keep going.

Jesus, you know how prone to fear I have been. I don't want fear to rule my decisions or keep me stuck in cycles of self-protection. Where fear says to stay small, help me choose your love that invites me to dream bigger and hold on to the promise that you are with me through it all.

NEWNESS

If anyone is in Christ, he is a new creation.
The old has passed away;
behold, the new has come.

1 CORINTHIANS 5:17 ESV

When you think of the reasons that Jesus came to earth, what comes to mind? Take some time to list them out whether in your mind or on paper. There are no right or wrong answers here; just let the thoughts flow out like a stream of consciousness. Once you see them laid out, you can evaluate your thoughts.

Does the list of reasons include anything personal to you, or is it all general and big picture? Do these things align with what you truly believe in your bones about God, or do they reflect the conditioning of your upbringing, culture, or church doctrine? It's probably a mix of both. May you take to heart the verse of the day, which states that "if anyone is in Christ, he is a new creation." Jesus came, not only to show us the way to the Father, but to make us new. He makes you new. You are a new creation in Christ!

Jesus, thank you for your sacrifice. Thank you for the incomparable love you displayed, and continue to display, in your merciful kindness. Thank you for making me new. I am not bound to sin; I am alive and free in you.

WHERE HE DWELLS

Splendor and majesty are before him;
strength and joy are in his dwelling place.

1 CHRONICLES 16:27 NIV

In the throne room of the King of heaven, there is more splendor and glory than we can imagine. Where he dwells, there is radiant light. The majesty of his presence brings everyone to their knees. When you consider that strength and joy are in his dwelling place, does it make you want to seek him?

The good news is that we have access to his presence here and now. We don't have to wait to experience his strength, grace, and joy. His perfect peace resides in the fellowship of Spirit to spirit. When we are joined to the Spirit of Christ, as Paul says in Romans 8, Christ is alive within us. May we be yielded to his love, living for his kingdom purposes, by the Spirit who directs us from within.

Jesus, there really is none like you. I can't wait until every blinder from my eyes is removed and I can see and know you fully even as I am fully known. Until that day, I will press into your presence and seek your kingdom first.

ABOVE ALL ELSE

Above all, love each other deeply,
because love covers over a multitude of sins.

1 PETER 4:8 NIV

No matter how many times we try and fail, no matter how many times we get it wrong, there is a way back to connection. Reparations are always made through love. This is not a love that makes excuses or seeks the easy way out. It's not a love that cannot admit its own failures.

Humble love that pushes past our comfort zones and pride reaches out to others. It takes responsibility and asks for help. It chooses vulnerability over control. It expands rather than contracts. This kind of deep love, the love that costs us something, is what covers over a multitude of sins and leads us back to connection with each other.

Jesus, thank you for the example of your living love that never gives up, never loses hope, and never stops pursuing us. I want to be more like you. Give me strength to choose humility over pride, compassion over self-protection, and softness over a hard heart.

INHERENT GOODNESS

Everything God created is good, and nothing
is to be rejected if it is received with thanksgiving.

1 Timothy 4:4 niv

When we become overly strict with ourselves and others,
we may set ourselves up for a major pendulum swing.
When we recognize that God does not deal with us in rigid
rules and does not try to manipulate us with his love, we
can be free of the fences that we so willingly build around
our understanding.

May we learn to see the beauty of what God has created
along with the different expressions of his goodness. Love
calls us to reach out of ourselves instead of staying within
the walls of our comfort. May we learn to love the liberty
that Christ has given us, for there is goodness all around
that we can receive with thankful hearts.

*Jesus, you are my liberator and my Savior. I don't want
to live so rigidly in my understanding of you and your
kingdom that I reduce it to a bunch of rules to follow. Your
kingdom values are principles to apply to my life. Help me,
Lord, to live with the fruit of your Spirit as I lean into your
liberating love.*

QUIET CONFIDENCE

"Your Father knows exactly what you need
even before you ask him!"

MATTHEW 6:8 NLT

For anyone who has ever felt overlooked or unseen,
for those who have gone without when others seem to
overflow in plenty, take Jesus' words to heart today. Our
Father knows exactly what we need even before we think
to ask him.

He will not let us go destitute. He will not ignore the cries
of our hearts. He reads our souls like open books and picks
up on every nuance and detail. There is more than enough
in his abundant kingdom to meet each of our needs. As we
approach him in prayer, let's take hope and take heart in
his knowledge of our situations.

*Jesus, thank you for being my advocate. You see every
need I have before I even realize it's there. You are not
blind to my problems or my hopes. I will not hold back my
heart from you even a little today.*

TRUE COMPETENCE

We don't see ourselves as capable enough to do anything in our own strength, for our true competence flows from God's empowering presence.

2 CORINTHIANS 3:5 TPT

Though we may have many gifts and talents to offer this world, there is one who is more able. Our strengths don't add a thing to his. Thankfully, that means that our weaknesses don't take away from his power at all, either.

Let's lean into the empowering presence of God and fill up on his grace and strength in every moment of need and every victory. We don't need to diminish our part, and we don't need to over-inflate it. True competence flows from God's Spirit at work within us. Praise God!

Jesus, you are my true competence. You are the one I rely on. When I am strong, you are stronger. When I am weak, you are still powerful. Move through me as I depend on you. You are my source in all things, for I originated in your heart.

FIRMLY PLACED

The Lord Yahweh is always faithful to place you on a firm foundation and guard you from the Evil One.

2 THESSALONIANS 3:3 TPT

Though we can choose how we will build our lives—the values we live by, the goals we aim to reach, the consistent effort we put in to get there—there will be times when the rug is pulled out from beneath us. Unexpected troubles like a diagnosis, a death, a broken heart, or a career change, will happen to each of us.

When this happens, we cannot rely on our strength to get us through. We cannot pretend to have the strength to stand when our legs are trembling. In these times, let's lean on the faithfulness of the Lord to place us on a firm foundation of his own making. We must let him be our defender and our advocate. He is powerful in grave-busting mercy and loyal in ever-flowing love.

Jesus, thank you for placing my feet on the firm foundation of your love when I cannot move myself. Thank you for being a sure foundation, a safe place of refuge, and all I need. I trust you.

LOOK TO CHRIST

See to it that no one takes you captive through hollow and deceptive philosophy, which depends on human tradition and the elemental spiritual forces of this world rather than on Christ.

COLOSSIANS 2:8 NIV

There is a better day coming than we can imagine. When Christ returns and every knee bows before him, he will make all things align in his limitless love. There will be final fulfillment of his promises, and he will break open our hope with the reality of his resurrection power.

We can taste and see the goodness of God through Christ right now. Let's look to Jesus more than we do any other teacher. With him is truth, life, and freedom. He is our ultimate authority, and he is our King. Let's not get distracted by insipid ideologies that focus on things Christ never did. He is the living expression of the Father, so let's look to him.

Jesus, I want my mind to be renewed in your living love. Please, break down the lies I have subtly bought into. I don't want to be so consumed with religion that I miss you. Teach me as I look to you.

HE DOES NO WRONG

"He is the Rock, his works are perfect,
and all his ways are just.
A faithful God who does no wrong,
upright and just is he."

DEUTERONOMY 32:4 NIV

God is not a liar. He is not a swindler. He is not an egomaniac. He is not vindictive. He is not a power-monger. He is not insecure. He is not any of the traits we see in others that diminish another's value or worth for their own sake. He is pure love.

With this in mind and knowing God does no wrong, can we recognize areas where we've assigned untrue attributes to God's character? He is limitless in mercy and kindness. He is mighty in justice. He does not throw sheep to wolves so that some might be saved. He cares about the least of these. He is powerful to save.

Jesus, you are perfect, and all your ways are just. I confess I have not believed that about you in every area. Refine my understanding in the lengths of your love. Transform my mind with your wonderful wisdom. Thank you.

UNDETERRED PERSPECTIVE

God has made everything beautiful for its own time. He has planted eternity in the human heart, but even so, people cannot see the whole scope of God's work from beginning to end.

ECCLESIASTES 3:11 NLT

If you feel you've been left behind by others, be encouraged by God's perfect timing today. If others are entering into new spheres of life you have been longing for, don't let envy cloud your vision. Your story is your own, and you are right on time.

We cannot see the scope of God's work, for we only see and know in part. He doesn't miss a detail, and he takes the whole picture into account. He has not forgotten you. If you are in a season of waiting, keep doing the work that is in front of you to do. It is not worthless; even the earth goes dormant in the winter. There is purpose in every season, and God is at work in the details of your life.

Jesus, I trust you with my life. Give me greater understanding of your timing, and may I see what you are doing in the cracks of my life as I live with intention. Encourage my heart in hope. May my eyes stay fixed on you as the perfecter of my faith.

RADIANT GLORY

This is the message we have heard from him
and declare to you: God is light;
in him there is no darkness at all.

1 JOHN 1:5 NIV

God's character will never change. There are no
interruptions to his nature. He is living love, full of radiant
light and giving life to all who are touched by his rays.
There is no darkness in him, for he exists in emanating
glory.

As we walk through dark valleys, God's light does not dim.
He sees everything clearly, and he will not let us stumble
as we depend on his leadership. He will carry us when
we have no strength to move. He will strengthen us when
we are hungry and tired. Though we cannot avoid the
darkness of the night seasons of life, stars shine bright on
the darkest nights. There is still light. He is still radiant.

*Jesus, when I cannot see the path in front of me, light the
way with your wisdom. Be my help and my guide when I
cannot sense a direction. I need you, I worship you, and I
am so grateful for your persistent presence in my life.*

JOINED TO JESUS

We have become his poetry, a re-created people that will fulfill the destiny he has given each of us, for we are joined to Jesus, the Anointed One. Even before we were born, God planned in advance our destiny and the good works we would do to fulfill it!

EPHESIANS 2:10 TPT

When we live our lives joined to Jesus, he weaves the stanzas of our days into a beautiful poem. Our lives are less like spreadsheets and more like works of art. May we take delight in the surprising ways that beauty shows up through his redemptive work in our lives.

There is so much good to do here and now. There is more than enough grace to help us through each challenge. There are solutions to the problems we face, and until they are made clear, we have the presence of God to help us persist and endure in love. May we have eyes to see how intricately we are woven into the fabric of his mercy.

Jesus, I take delight in your work in my life. Thank you for pursuing me with purpose and for loving me to life again and again in your presence. You are my joy, and my life is your masterpiece. May you be glorified in it.

LET THE LORD BUILD

Unless the LORD builds the house,
the builders labor in vain.
Unless the LORD watches over the city,
the guards stand watch in vain.

PSALM 127:1 NIV

What drives your work ethic? Is it fear of not having enough? Is your motivation to provide for your family while making an impact on your community? Is it to fuel the dreams you hope to accomplish one day? Whatever the answer, God's grace is with you to help you build. His mercy is present to watch over your home and community.

Where fear drives you, take time to reevaluate and submit to the provision of the Lord. Rest is as important to your success as hard work. Consistent showing up and follow-through, balanced with play, rest, and pleasure, will help your life reflect the mercy of God. He is able to do far more than you can alone, so partner with him and trust him to fill in the gaps you miss.

Jesus, empower me with your grace. Help me build a life that glorifies you and exemplifies your love. I want to invest in my relationships as much as my bank account. Lead me with your wisdom and watch over me with your mercy.

LIBERATED LIVING

It is for freedom that Christ has set us free.
Stand firm, then, and do not let yourselves
be burdened again by a yoke of slavery.

GALATIANS 5:1 NIV

In John 8, Jesus says that when we sin, we are not free. He goes on to say, "If the Son sets you free, you will be free indeed" (John 8:26). We should live as the children of God that we are and be free. When we let sin become our master once more, we are burdened again by a yoke of slavery that he already liberated us from.

When love is our motivation, it frees us from fear, shame, and limitations, and we align with the kingdom values of Christ. When we live with mercy that expands our borders, compassion that reaches out of our comfort zones, and wisdom that sets clear boundaries to keep our values in place, we practice the liberty of his love.

Jesus, thank you for the freedom you have given me. I will not let shame keep me stuck in cycles of sin you have already freed me from. I step into your liberating love, and I choose connection with you and others.

SHARP TRUTH

The word of God is alive and active. Sharper than any double-edged sword, it penetrates even to dividing soul and spirit, joints and marrow; it judges the thoughts and attitudes of the heart.

HEBREWS 4:12 NIV

The Word of God is full of instructive wisdom. In the first chapter and verse of John, Jesus is referred to as the Word. "In the beginning was the Word, and the Word was with God, and the Word was God."

Jesus is alive and active. He is sharper than any double-edged sword, and he can pierce the deepest parts of our hearts to separate soul and spirit. He judges the thoughts and attitudes of our hearts. He speaks, and there is clarity. He moves, and we are moved. There is a deep knowing in his wisdom. He gives focus to our confusion, and he shines light on the shadows of our understanding so that we can perceive his will.

Jesus, thank you for the truth of your living Spirit in my life. Move in me. Pierce me with your truth, and separate the lies I have believed, the misconceptions and misunderstandings, from your unrelenting reality.

MAY

"The LORD himself will fight for you.
Just stay calm."

EXODUS 14:14 NLT

PURSUED BY PEACE

Let the peace that Christ gives control your thinking, because you were all called together in one body to have peace. Always be thankful.

Colossians 3:15 NCV

Jesus is known as the Prince of Peace. He is full of clarity and calm, and he cannot be moved by the hectic world that rushes to conclusions and is quick to shut down other points of view. His peace unifies; it does not divide. It promotes understanding between people with compassion and empathy. It is kind, merciful, and true.

Let this peace, the peace of Christ, rule over your thoughts. Be a promoter of peace through lovingkindness. Slow down your reactions when you find yourself jumping to judge someone you have not taken the time to listen to. May love guard your heart. May peace keep your mind fixed on the values of the kingdom of Christ that never expire or grow stale.

Jesus, thank you for the peace I have in your presence. Calm my anxious thoughts. Meet me with your clarifying wisdom that slows down my heart and beats with steady measure. I trust you, and I yield to your ways over my own.

HEALTHY GROWTH

People who work for peace in a peaceful way
plant a good crop of right-living.

JAMES 3:18 NCV

The wisdom of God is found in people who work for peace. Peace-promoting behaviors do not sway or give under the pressure of others' shouting voices. Peacemakers continue to reach out in the merciful kindness of God and do not give up easily.

There is a beautiful harvest of righteousness that comes from the labor of promoting peace. May we give ourselves to it and not grow weary. When we follow the lead of Jesus, we walk the pathways of his kingdom that are lined with heavenly wisdom. Let's keep loving, pursuing peace, and doing what is right in the eyes of the Lord.

Jesus, thank you for your example of peace that does not display prejudice or hypocrisy. Thank you for the purity of your wisdom that is humble and teachable. I am your willing student, follower, and friend.

WHOLE-HEARTED SEARCHING

"You will seek me and find me
when you seek me with all your heart."

JEREMIAH 29:13 NIV

If we truly want something, we will do what it takes to attain it. Our desires do not only keep us dreaming; they motivate us to pursue the reality of those dreams. Let's make sure that we're actually working toward what we want in life. With intention and consistency, as we keep showing up and putting in the work, we will find what we're looking for.

God said that when we seek him with all our hearts, we will find him. How much attention do we give to him? How much time do we set aside for praying, meditating on his Word, and fellowshipping with him in his presence? When we seek him, we will find him. Let's do it today.

Jesus, I seek you today with all my heart. I am open to receiving your instruction and your wisdom. I want to know you more. I want to worship you in spirit and in truth. Reveal yourself to me as I look for you.

IN HIS CARE

You gave me life and showed me kindness,
and in your care you watched over my life.

JOB 10:12 NCV

What a glorious God we have been created by! In his image, the image in which we are made, we find kindness that fuels our peace and joy. In his care, we are watched over and kept close in his loyal love. He is the source of our very lives, and he does not withhold his mercy from any who look to him for help.

What are you worried about today? Is there a weariness that you just can't shake? Find kindness in the fellowship of the Spirit of God. He is with you now; he is ready to listen and help. He cares for you more than you can imagine. His marvelous mercy is ready to relieve your heavy heart with miracles of tender kindness. Press in, turn your attention to him, and find that he cares so tenderly for you.

Jesus, thank you for your presence through your Spirit. Lift the heaviness of my anxieties and the load of my weariness. I long for rest in your presence, for rejuvenation in your joy, and for relief in your love. Show me how deeply you care for me.

SECRET RICHES

"I will give you hidden treasures,
riches stored in secret places,
so that you may know that I am the Lord,
the God of Israel, who summons you by name."

Isaiah 45:3 niv

No matter in what season of the soul you find yourself,
there are treasures to be unearthed and joys to be
discovered. There is a storehouse of riches that never run
out in the kingdom of our God. He is the God who meets
us with the mercy of his heart over and over again. There is
wisdom to instruct us, beauty to leave us breathless in awe,
and deep peace to settle our hearts.

Wherever you are today, God is with you. He is full of
loyal love to pour over and into you. He is not lacking in
anything! Do you need strength? He has grace for you. Do
you need vision? He has wisdom to impart. Do you need
hope? He has faithfulness to encourage you. Feast on the
fullness of his presence, and you will find secret riches to
surprise you.

*Jesus, reveal your hidden treasures in my life today. I know
you grow glorious gardens even from the rubble of my
story. I want to feast on your faithfulness today. Open my
eyes and show me the gifts you offer.*

EVERYTHING MADE CLEAR

"Nothing is hidden that will not be made manifest,
nor is anything secret that will not be known
and come to light."

LUKE 8:17 ESV

Though we live in a world full of mysteries still being
uncovered, God is not surprised by anything. He sees
everything clearly. One day, we will also see it that way in
the fullness of the light of his glory. Know this: no secret
you try to keep hidden will stay that way forever. Live with
integrity, honesty, humility, and mercy. You won't regret it
if you do.

Don't forget the marvelous mercy of God that covers your
sin and shame. In him, everything wrong will be made right.
He is your salvation and covering. His resurrection power
is enough to break the power of death; surely it is strong
enough to set you free from your fears! When you live in
the light, as God is in the light, you have nothing to be
afraid of and certainly nothing to hide.

*Jesus, thank you for the power of your redemption in my
life. I want to live with integrity and not keep anything
hidden in shame or fear. I know your love liberates me. As
I seek restoration in areas where I desperately need it, I
know you will help me.*

DIRECTED BY LOVE

By day the LORD directs his love,
at night his song is with me—
a prayer to the God of my life.

PSALM 42:8 NIV

When the Lord directs his love, he sends its endless flow to cascade over us. None of us can escape its power. Have you ever thought about the fact that God's love is a never-ending flow? It reaches us, washes over us, and covers us all the days of our lives.

Take a moment to focus your attention on the nearness of his love. It meets you with abundance right where you are this moment. He sings over you with songs of delighted affection. Oh, how he loves you! He is more concerned about you than what you do. He is full of compassion toward you. He has not left you, nor will he. He is here, now, with the generosity of his merciful kindness. He never lets up, and he will never let you go.

Jesus, thank you for your overwhelming love for me. No matter how many times I fail, or others fail me, you never will. Direct my attention back to your love when I am distracted by disappointment. I love you.

LOOSEN YOUR GRIP

"If you try to hang on to your life, you will lose it.
But if you give up your life for my sake, you will save it."

MATTHEW 16:25 NLT

When we hold too tightly to our ideas of what the future will look like, we will be disappointed. Nothing ever turns out exactly as we expect. We must leave room for God to work through the unexpected trials of life as much as he does through the hard-won victories.

When we loosen our grip on our lives and give up the illusion of controlling every facet of our futures, we make room for confident trust in God's faithfulness. Let's be flexible in our expectations, and at the same time, be completely confident in God's ability. He is able to do much more than we could think or imagine asking for.

Jesus, I let go of the need to control how I think my life should go. I cannot escape the unknowns that will meet me on my path, but you are not surprised by a single one of them. I trust you to lead me, and I willingly submit to your guidance through it all.

IT'S POSSIBLE

I can do everything through Christ,
who gives me strength.

PHILIPPIANS 4:13 NLT

In our humanity, we will reach our limits over and over again. We need rest and renewal as part of our lives. Sometimes, unexpected illnesses take us out of our normal routines, and our bodies aren't able to do what they once could. Our stamina may suffer. We need rest. We were not made to push ourselves to the breaking point. It is not holy to work ourselves into the ground.

We need not get ahead of ourselves and be overwhelmed by the great scope of what we could not imagine accomplishing today. We can focus on what is ours to do today. What should the next small step be? Lean into the wisdom and strength of Christ who will help you face each step as it comes. You can do it through him.

Jesus, thank you for being with me in the menial steps as much as you are in the big leaps of life. I need your grace and strength to help me focus on what is mine to do today. Please, give me vision and focus; be my help. Thank you.

WISDOM'S BENEFITS

Wise words bring many benefits,
and hard work brings rewards.

PROVERBS 12:14 NLT

The wisdom of God is not only found in the Scriptures. It is found in the practical compassion of a friend reaching out. It is found in a stranger's helping hand. It is found in caring for others. Wisdom does not lead us away from the simple truth of Jesus; it helps us walk it out in our lives.

When was the last time wise words struck you to the core and shifted your perspective? It could be a big shift or a small, subtle one. Any movement in peace, compassion, joy, solidarity, or grounded trust boasts of the wisdom of the kingdom of God. There is a reward for all who sow seeds of peace. There is a harvest for those who till the fields of righteousness. Let wisdom coupled with hard work direct your focus today.

Jesus, thank you for the practicality of your wisdom. What you teach is not complicated. What you instruct is not out of my reach. I lean into your grace and step forward with a willing heart. With ready hands, I will partner with your purposes.

REJOICE IN REFUGE

Let all who take refuge in you rejoice;
let them sing joyful praises forever.
Spread your protection over them,
that all who love your name may be filled with joy.

PSALM 5:11 NLT

There is enough going on in the world that causes us to mourn. There are nations and tribes at war; divisions and active injustices happen around us. God did not promise that we would not experience pain, suffering, or loss. Instead, he promises to be with us through them, to deliver us, and to be our loving leader through it all.

Where do you find your refuge? Where do you experience peace? When the worries of this life are too much to bear, where do you put them? Let's pray, not only for our own relief and protection, but for the same for others who are suffering. Let's look for ways to further the kingdom of God by spreading our protection over the vulnerable when we are able. The relief of others will turn to rejoicing, and we will share in their joy.

Jesus, I have found relief and refreshment in your presence. I pray for those who have no escape today. Please, be their covering and their help. Spread your wings over them. Show me how I can partner with you in doing the same. Help me bring joy to those who have been burdened down by mourning.

LOOK AROUND

Ever since the world was created, people have seen the earth and sky. Through everything God made, they can clearly see his invisible qualities—his eternal power and divine nature. So they have no excuse for not knowing God.

ROMANS 1:20 NLT

Psalm 19 says, "The heavens proclaim the glory of God. The skies display his craftsmanship. Day after day they continue to speak...their voice is never heard. Yet their message has gone throughout the earth, and their words to all the world."

When was the last time you spent time in nature and paid attention to the wonders of creation around you? Whether it was yesterday or ten years ago, may you be encouraged to notice the way the sunlight plays with the objects it touches, leaving pockets of shadows, or how the wind dances through the limbs of trees and their leaves. Look for the clues of God's workmanship. It is out in plain sight for all to see!

Jesus, thank you for the beauty of your creation. May I know you more, love you more, and seek you more because of what I take notice of in nature today. You are such a creative God. Thank you for sharing your work with us.

SEALED BY LOVE

Place me like a seal over your heart, like a seal on your arm; for love is as strong as death, its jealousy unyielding as the grave. It burns like blazing fire, like a mighty flame.

SONG OF SOLOMON 8:6 NIV

The love of God is like a blazing inferno that overtakes drought-stricken lands. It will not relent. It is like mighty ocean waters that rise with the force of a tsunami, covering all in its path. However, love does not destroy the way fires and floods do. His love overtakes everything it touches, but it brings life instead of death.

This fierce love is the same love that reaches you today. It is not wimpy or weak. It is not unsure or finicky. It is steady, it is strong, and it is more than enough for all your needs. Let the love of God sweep through you. Do not fight; surrender to it. There is more than enough love, joy, peace, patience, kindness, and power—all the things you are looking for—in its depths.

Jesus, thank you for letting love compel you. It took you beyond the bounds of heaven, to the earth, and to the grave, and ultimately to your throne again. I want to be fueled by your passion, Lord. Set me ablaze for you and your purposes.

CONFIDENCE IN CRISIS

God is your confidence in times of crisis,
keeping your heart at rest in every situation.

PROVERBS 3:26 TPT

When crisis strikes, may God be your confidence. When unavoidable trouble comes knocking, may you rest your heart in God's peace. Jesus instructed us not to worry about anything, for the Father will provide for all our needs. This is true both in times of famine and feasting.

Let's lean into the grace-filled strength of our faithful God and let his Spirit build up our hope and keep our hearts firmly tethered to his mercy. Whatever crisis you are facing today, turn to God. Trust him to get you through. He will. Throw all your cares on him; he'll carry their weight. Declare his faithfulness over your life, for he won't ever stop being faithful. He is not just great. No, he is infinitely better than you can imagine.

Jesus, you are my confidence in crisis. You are the one I turn to when I have nowhere else to turn. I trust you to continue to work out your love in my life, no matter what it looks like now. I know you are faithful, so I will continue to trust you.

PURE PROMISES

The Lord's promises are pure,
like silver refined in a furnace,
purified seven times over.

PSALM 12:6 NLT

You will never find a better promise keeper than the Lord
your God. He does not grow weak or weary, and he never
has reason to fear. He is perfect peace and full of truth and
righteousness. He is powerful to save. He always sees the
end from the beginning. He hasn't lost sight of a single
detail of what he has said, and he certainly won't fail to
follow through on his word.

The Lord's promises are purer than any we could ever
make. He has no hidden motive. He is full of light and life,
and he will continue to reveal his goodness in the ways that
his merciful miracles work out in our lives and in the world.

Jesus, thank you for the purity of your love and truth.
There are no power plays in your kingdom. You are
humble, you are merciful, and you are righteous. You
won't stop being the pure and shining one. I trust you to
fulfill every promise you have made.

EASILY IDENTIFIABLE

"Just as you can identify a tree by its fruit,
so you can identify people by their actions."

MATTHEW 7:20 NLT

When we take time to learn the foliage and fruit of the lands we dwell in, we can easily identify what we find in nature. An oak tree will always look like an oak tree. A magnolia bud will never be anything but a magnolia.

Just as we do in nature, so can we learn the fruit of the kingdom of Christ. We have been told how to look for evidence of the fruit of the Spirit in our lives: "love, joy, peace, patience, kindness, goodness, faithfulness, gentleness, and self-control" (Galatians 5:22-23). It is not a mystery to identify those who live according to the kingdom of Christ. The fruit of their actions will be evidence enough.

Jesus, thank you for your simple wisdom that instructs so clearly. Firstly, I want my life to exemplify your Spirit's fruit. That is all I can truly control. Secondly, I am grateful I am not at a loss to identify those who truly want to live for you as well.

NOURISHED BY MERCY

"I love each of you with the same love that
the Father loves me. You must continually
let my love nourish your hearts."

JOHN 15:9 TPT

We are each loved with the same love that the Father has
for his son, Jesus Christ. We are co-heirs with Christ and
children of the living God. Are we being nourished by this
love, or are we seeking to fill our bellies elsewhere?

As we take time to fellowship with Jesus through prayer,
we will find that his presence is near and moving both
within us and around us. His love is the only thing strong
enough to build our identities upon. There is no firmer
foundation, no surer place to be found, than on the solid
rock of his merciful kindness.

*Jesus, I take time right now to focus my attention on your
living love. Your mercy is better than my own limited love,
and yet even with my limits, nothing is wasted in your
hands. Nourish me with your kindness. Strengthen me in
the truth of who you say that I am.*

LIFTED BY THE LORD

Humble yourselves before the Lord,
and he will lift you up.

JAMES 4:10 NIV

When we are humble before the Lord, we recognize our total dependence on God for everything. In his sermon on the mount, Jesus said, "Blessed are the poor in spirit, for theirs is the kingdom of heaven" (Matthew 5:3). He also declared, "Blessed are the meek, for they will inherit the earth" (Matthew 5:5).

When we are gentle and flexible, not demanding anything as our own, as the proud do, we are able to receive whatever God gives us. Let us not resist what he so freely offers us. Instead, let's humble ourselves before him, and he will lift us up. He has everything we need, and he always treats us with honor. May we also lift up the humble and honor each person in their humanity as Christ does with us.

Jesus, thank you for your persistent kindness which meets me in every season of my soul and life. You never turn away in disgust. You don't shrink back in horror. You know me, you love me, and you lift me up. Thank you.

NEW THINGS COMING

"Look at the new thing I am going to do.
It is already happening. Don't you see it?
I will make a road in the desert
and rivers in the dry land."

ISAIAH 43:19 NCV

There is no terrain too wild that God cannot tame it. There is no human heart so cold that God cannot melt with his tender and persistent love. There is no worry so all-consuming that God cannot break through the fear with the power of his perfect peace. He settles our anxieties and leads us in confidence, and he won't ever change.

God is always up to something new. He is constantly creating new opportunities, and we can take heart and take hope in his faithful mercy at work in every area of our lives. He is with us in the muddy trenches of war as much as he is in the sun-filled fields of peace. Let us look to him, for he is making a way where there was none before.

Jesus, thank you for being a way maker. In all you do, you move in loyal love. I want to see where you are opening a door where there were only walls before. Give me eyes to see; I am following your lead.

KEEP SEARCHING

I will show my love to those who passionately love me.
For they will search and search continually
until they find me.

PROVERBS 8:17 TPT

When we search for the Lord, we will find him. Jesus
himself said so. In Matthew 7:8, he says, "Every persistent
seeker will discover what he longs for. And everyone who
knocks persistently will one day find an open door."

If you have grown weary in your search for God and his
wisdom, may you find fresh courage to keep pursuing him
today. He is already at work within and around you. May
your eyes be open to the myriad of miracles and beauty
in the world around you. May your love burn hotter as
you catch glimpses of his glory already so close at hand.
You do not need to go to the ends of the earth to find his
handiwork; just look in the mirror. You will see it.

*Jesus, thank you for promising that I'll find what I'm
looking for. I know true satisfaction is found in you, and I
want to know the depth of fullness that my heart longs for.
Reveal yourself to me right where I am in life today. My
eyes are open.*

EVERY MOMENT

Because you are close to me and always available,
my confidence will never be shaken,
for I experience your wrap-around presence
every moment.

PSALM 16:8 TPT

If you are able, read the verse of the day aloud and perhaps more than once. Let your voice declare this Scripture until it sinks deep into your consciousness, and you feel your heart confirming its message.

The wrap-around presence of the Lord surrounds you even now. Every moment of every day, the Spirit of God is with you. No matter how you have felt or what you have doubted, the faithfulness of God is unwavering. He is close to you and always available. May your confidence grow stronger as you remind yourself of his unshakeable love.

Jesus, thank you for the fullness of your presence available to me every second. I cannot even fathom this possibility, but I believe that your Word is true. In this moment, surround me with the tangible peace of your presence. Awaken my heart in your lifegiving love.

HOLY WORK

Work at living in peace with everyone,
and work at living a holy life,
for those who are not holy
will not see the Lord.

HEBREWS 12:14 NLT

There is a reason that the instruction of living at peace and living a holy life are described as being worked for. There is no final destination of being at peace. There is no guarantee that your integrity will not be upset by challenges at any moment. When we work at living at peace with everyone, and we work at living a holy life, it leaves room for the process of it. When we live, move, and breathe with intention, we are doing the work of moving toward that goal.

What intentions do you have set for your days? If promoting peace is not one, perhaps make room for growth there. If holiness has not been a high value, seek the Lord for his help in that area. He is full of patient love to guide you and strengthen you in purpose, motivation, and follow-through.

Jesus, thank you for the example you set in promoting peace and love in your life. I want to be holy as you were in your humanity. Give me grit and grace to grow in these areas as I follow you.

WHAT IS PRODUCED

The Holy Spirit produces this kind of fruit
in our lives: love, joy, peace, patience,
kindness, goodness, faithfulness.

GALATIANS 5.22 NLT

Where can you see the fruit of the Holy Spirit alive and
active in your life? Can you recognize where love abounds,
joy rises, peace is pursued, patience is planted, kindness is
extended, goodness is present, and faithfulness abounds?

The work of God reveals the values of his kingdom. His
mercy renews life where there once were ashes. It is
important to recognize the seasons we're in, but it is also
important to recognize where the fruit of his presence is
alive and active. He is always abundant in the fullness of his
lifegiving power. May we have eyes to see and ears to hear
what the Spirit is doing and saying.

*Jesus, I'm grateful that there is room in your kingdom
for your fruit to show up in unexpected areas of my life.
You are cultivating a garden rather than duplicating a
blueprint. I love that! May I have the same approach to
building in my own life and sphere of influence.*

RICH IN KINDNESS

He is so rich in kindness and grace
that he purchased our freedom with the
blood of his Son and forgave our sins.

EPHESIANS 1:7 NLT

No matter how you feel about your current life situation, you can know the exceeding goodness of God's kindness and grace extending toward you now. He has offered you forgiveness and purchased your freedom. Jesus Christ, the same resurrected one who broke the chains of sin and death, is your Savior today.

May you take hold of the kindness that God offers you. He will not draw back as you reach for him. May his glorious grace be your strength and confidence as you surrender to the overwhelming tide of his affection. What he has forgiven, agree to forgive. Let yourself off the hook of judgment where he has declared your freedom. What he has forgiven in you, release in compassion to others. There is an abundance of kindness and grace in his presence, and it will never run dry.

Jesus, I am undone at the overwhelming reality of your lovingkindness. It is my salvation and my strength. It is my peace and my joy. Thank you!

WAIT ON THE LORD

I wait for the LORD,
my whole being waits,
and in his word I put my hope.

PSALM 130:5 NIV

When we wait on the Lord, we renew our strength. When we wait for him to rise on our behalf, lead us through the valley of the shadow of death, and bring us into the open plains of his favor, we rely on his leadership.

Wait on the Lord. Let your whole being wait. Quiet your soul. Turn your attention to him and offer him the thoughts of your mind. His Word is full of clarity for your confusion. His wisdom is simple, but it is not always the path of least resistance. Trust him. He will not fail to guide you with his strong right hand and the confidence of his faithfulness. Wait on him.

Jesus, I trust you more than the possibilities that anxiety swirls within me. I trust you more than my experience, more than my hopes, and more than anything. I wait on you, and as I do, wrap around me with your presence. Speak, Lord; I am listening.

ONLY JESUS

There is salvation in no one else! God has given no other name under heaven by which we must be saved.

ACTS 4:12 NLT

Jesus is the way to the Father. He is the open door we walk through to enter the fullness of the Father's presence. We come through his gate and leave all our shame at the door. Jesus has taken the weight of our sin, our fears, and our greatest failings. When we come to him, he clothes us in the robes of his own righteousness so we can approach the Father.

When we fellowship with Jesus, we fellowship with the Father. When we fellowship with the Spirit, we fellowship with Jesus. We fellowship with Father, Son, and Spirit. There is fullness of acceptance and salvation through Christ. There is no more to do, to be, to act on, then to come through him. Will we trust his holy Word and his open invitation?

Jesus, no one under heaven or above the earth can represent the Father more fully than you do. I long to know you more and to be unencumbered by fear or shame. I walk to you and through you in the confidence of your finished work and resurrection power. You are my God, and I worship you.

DELIGHTED BY WEAKNESS

I'm not defeated by my weakness, but delighted! For when I feel my weakness and endure mistreatment— when I'm surrounded with troubles on every side and face persecution because of my love for Christ—I am made yet stronger.

2 CORINTHIANS 12:10 TPT

When was the last time you were delighted by your weakness? In our humanity, it is not a normal reaction to take joy in our limitations. Paul, however, made a practice of counting his weaknesses as well as his strengths. He knew that he had access to the power of God through his Spirit as much in his frailty as he did in his strength.

What areas of weakness have you been beating yourself up for? May you find fresh perspective in Paul's words today. Instead of being defeated, let yourself wonder at what delight would look like. When you endure mistreatment and troubles close in on you, let the love of Christ be the strength that directs your focus. Look for opportunities of gratitude even in the cracks of your situation. There, you will find God's grace still at work.

Jesus, thank you for the promise of your redemption in my life. I lean into your grace as I seek to reframe my weakness as an opportunity for your mercy to do its work in me. Reveal your strength in my weakness, Lord.

GODLY WEALTH

True godliness with contentment
is itself great wealth.

1 TIMOTHY 6:6 NLT

True wealth that lasts in the kingdom of God is not found our bank accounts or net worth. There is nothing wrong with having resources and working hard, for we can then be generous and share what we have with others. Money is not a moral thing; it is a tool. It should not be our main goal in life. It is fleeting, and we cannot take it with us when our souls depart this earth.

There is a soul's wealth that we can build no matter what we do or don't have in physical resources. When we cultivate gratitude that finds satisfaction in what we already have, we can focus on the greater things of the kingdom. May we find ourselves doing the Lord's work, promoting the values of his ways, and following after Christ in all we do.

Jesus, I know true wealth is found in you. I don't want to be deceived into thinking what I have represents how you feel about me. I don't want more stuff; I want more of you! I know you love us all the same in the overabundance of your merciful kindness. May I not judge myself or others based on what we have or do not have.

YET AGAIN

Why am I discouraged? Why is my heart so sad?
I will put my hope in God! I will praise him again—
my Savior and my God!

PSALM 42:11 NLT

When you find yourself discouraged, which we all will at one time or another, you have a choice. It is not some moral failing that you have committed. It is not a sin to be disheartened. It is not a failure to be depressed. When you find yourself in this space, you can still choose to put your hope in God. You can still choose to trust him.

In the middle of a moonless night, you can't discern what is around you. God sees everything clearly. Trust him to guard you, keep you, and guide you. He will not let you down. He will not fail, for his love never fails. He is with you even when you cannot sense his nearness. Dare to put your hope in him and trust him to do what you cannot.

Jesus, you are my holy hope, my consistent confidence, and my trustworthy truth. I cling to you even when I cannot make sense of my surroundings. I will put my hope in you. I will still praise you, my Savior and my God.

NEVER WASTED

My dear brothers and sisters, stand strong. Do not let anything move you. Always give yourselves fully to the work of the Lord, because you know that your work in the Lord is never wasted.

1 CORINTHIANS 15:58 NCV

Everything you do in love, peace, joy, and devotion to the Lord is counted, recorded, and remembered by him. He will not forget a single movement of mercy. He keeps your kindnesses in mind. When you are tempted to throw in the towel and give up, remember that he is not finished working out his mercy in your story.

Stand strong, sister. Keep going. Keep choosing the better way—the path of love. Keep doing what you know is right. Do not be afraid to follow the Lord into the great unknown of things. Where he leads, you can trust him. Where he goes, you can be sure he will not abandon you. Nothing is ever wasted, and his work is strong and sure.

Jesus, when I am tempted to give up on your ways, remind me of your love that never gives up on anyone. Fill me with the refreshing waters of your wise mercy. As I lean in to hear your voice, I trust I won't miss it. Thank you.

HIGHEST AIM

Dear friends, let us love one another, for love comes from God. Everyone who loves has been born of God and knows God.

1 John 4:7 NIV

There is no greater objective in this life than to love well. Just as we are loved, so should we seek to love others. How does Christ love us? Constantly, completely, and powerfully. It does not nitpick or put us down. It does not just point out our flaws and failures. Even in correction, the love of Christ is lifegiving, kind, and fruitful. It expands rather than contracts. It makes space instead of limiting us. It is full of freedom, joy, and peace.

May we seek to love others with the expansive mercy of Christ. As Corinthians says, may his love fuel our passion. May we give it freely just as Christ has lavished his love upon us without measure. We don't need to meter it out or keep track of what is owed. The love of God keeps no record of wrongs. Let us live with love as our highest priority and aim, for it is who God is and what he is made of.

Jesus, I want to love as you love. I want to be transformed into your likeness and shine the radiant light of your glory as the moon reflects the sun. Help me to love others the way that you do, purely and radically, without finding fault.

JUNE

Listen to my voice in the morning, Lord.
Each morning I bring my requests to you
and wait expectantly.

Psalm 5:3 nlt

INWARD RENEWAL

We do not lose heart. Though outwardly we are wasting away, yet inwardly we are being renewed day by day.

2 CORINTHIANS 4:16 NIV

Even when our bodies rebel against our wishes, even when we do not have the physical strength we once did or hoped we would, we can always be renewed inwardly. Our inner beings are fed by the never-ending flow of God's mighty mercy. It is our strength, our source, and our power. There is more life yet for us!

May you find your heart, soul, mind, and spirit renewed in the Spirit's fellowship today. May you be filled to overflowing with the love of his heart, the delight of his affection, and the peace of his steady nature. He has not changed, and he will not. He is the same powerful God you have trusted. Instead of focusing on what you cannot do today, let the Lord meet you in the expanse of your inner being.

Jesus, thank you for spirit-to-Spirit fellowship with you. Fill me, encourage me, and shift my limited perspective to see what you do. I want to know you more, to be renewed and refreshed in your presence, and to hope in ways I had forgotten I could. Thank you.

SPIRIT POWER

"You will receive power
when the Holy Spirit comes on you."

ACTS 1:8 NIV

Jesus instructed his disciples to stay in Jerusalem until the gift of the Father had been given to them. He had promised them the Holy Spirit. When Jesus left them, there was a period of waiting. Jesus did not immediately send the Spirit; the disciples had to wait for it, and they did. They waited with intercession and by gathering in community.

Is there something you have been waiting on? We live in an age of instant gratification, and it's easy to forget the value and power of the in-between. Do not give up. Seek community and fellowship with those who will encourage you to keep going. Keep seeking, keep praying, and keep meeting with those of like mind. In the meantime, know that the power of the Spirit is available to you today.

Jesus, thank you for the power of your promises. You are always faithful to fulfill them. I trust you, and I will not lose heart while waiting. Holy Spirit, fill me with the power of your presence today and build me up in your love.

IT ALL BELONGS

There is a time to cry and a time to laugh.
There is a time to be sad and a time to dance.

ECCLESIASTES 3:4 NCV

Have you ever felt as if sadness should not be part of your spirituality? Do you struggle to be open about your sorrows with others? Ecclesiastes holds the spectrum of human experience. "There is a time to cry and a time to laugh." None of us can escape seasons of grief and mourning, but we will not miss out on seasons of joy and peace either.

Whatever day you are having, whatever season you are in, know this: it all belongs. Life is not binary; often the *both* and the *in-between* exist in tense tandem. We can be incredibly sad and at the same time be happy for others. We can be relieved and yet mourn a deep loss. Let it be what it is and invite the Lord into it. He will comfort and strengthen you. He will celebrate with you and fill you with peace. Everything you are and everything you experience has a place with him.

Jesus, thank you for your friendship and fellowship. Be with me in my current season. May I know the overwhelming goodness of your love, no matter what I am walking through or dancing upon.

WHAT HE WANTED

God decided in advance to adopt us into his own family by bringing us to himself through Jesus Christ. This is what he wanted to do, and it gave him great pleasure.

EPHESIANS 1:5 NLT

It has always been in God's heart to adopt us into his family. We were never meant to live without his love covering us. We are made whole in his mercy. We each have a place that can never be taken by another in the kingdom of our God.

Do you know that God takes pleasure in calling you his child? Are you convinced of his delight over you? May the lies of shame be silenced in his presence today. May you know how wonderfully he has created you and how thoroughly he loves you, not because of what you do, but because of who you are. You are loved. You are found. You have a forever home in him.

Jesus, I cannot quite comprehend that you would want to adopt me as your own. Still, I believe I am yours and you delight in me. Speak your words of life over my heart again and fill me with the purity of your love.

IN HIS PRESENCE

"My presence will go with you,
and I will give you rest."

Exodus 33:14 esv

When God calls you forward, he promises to go with you. When life's unexpected trials come barging in and you cannot escape, you must walk through them. God promises to be with you and give you rest along the way. The peace of his presence is your plentiful portion in every season of the soul.

May you find rest in the presence of your Savior today. May peace settle the anxieties of your heart. May you know his perfect love that drives out fear. May he lead you beside still waters of refreshment and restore your soul. You are not alone. You are never alone.

Jesus, thank you for the promise of your presence in every moment and situation. I trust you when I cannot make any sense of my life. I trust you when I cannot gain my bearings. Wise One, lead me, keep me, and fill me with your expansive goodness. I rely on you.

LAW OF LOVE

Love completes the laws of God. All of the law can be summarized in one grand statement: "Demonstrate love to your neighbor, even as you care for and love yourself."

GALATIANS 5:14 TPT

The law of love that Jesus proclaimed as the highest way to live is as applicable today as it was when he first spoke it. It's also important to remember that love does not deny our needs. It doesn't ignore the importance of maintaining rhythms of rest within our busy schedules. It does not neglect boundaries that allow us to protect our peace.

In the same way we love and care for ourselves, we should demonstrate love and care to others. We give ourselves the benefit of the doubt because we know our own intentions. Do we judge others harshly, or do we offer room for their own well-meaning intentions? May we love with the same love of Jesus and follow his example in all we do. Love is the highest law, and it is the completion of the laws of God.

Jesus, I choose to follow your path of love in my life. I choose to extend mercy where I am tempted to withdraw in judgment or apathy. I lean on you, Lord. Teach me how to love myself well and to love others in the same generous manner.

ADVANCING IN FAITH

Now is the time for us to progress beyond the basic message of Christ and advance into perfection. The foundation has already been laid for us to build upon: turning away from our dead works to embrace faith in God.

HEBREWS 6:1 TPT

We do not gain favor with God by keeping religious laws and traditions. We do not serve others in order to garner more influence with God. Christ is our favor. Through him, we already have the open invitation of fellowship with the Father.

As children progress from milk to solid foods and from supervised play to independent play, so do we also gain more freedom and choice in our spiritual growth. God is our Father, and he is also our teacher. God is an advisor who will never force us to act in any particular way. He does not force our hand. May we press into obedient trust more and more as we rely on his faithfulness, for he will never fail us.

Jesus, thank you for the acceptance I have found in your presence. I am humbled to be a part of your family. Teach me and empower me with your grace to live with liberty, truth, justice, and mercy as hallmarks of my lifestyle. I press on in faith, and I believe you will do better things than I can imagine.

THE WAITING PRINCIPLE

The LORD must wait for you to come to him,
so he can show you his love and compassion.
For the LORD is a faithful God.
Blessed are those who wait for his help.

ISAIAH 30:18 NLT

In seasons of waiting, do you continue to press into the presence of God? Do you ask him for what you do not have? Do you rely on his help to persevere through hardship and trial? God's love is stronger than the grave, and he will not neglect to cover you with the power of his mercy whenever you come to him.

The Lord waits for us to approach him, but we also wait on his help after we do. If you find yourself in the in-between of promise and fulfillment, do not despair. It is not a sign of your failure or lack of faith; it is a part of the process. Trust him. Continue to pray, ask, and seek. Wait on his help. He will not let you down.

Jesus, remind me of your present love and compassion when I grow tired in the waiting seasons. Give me eyes to see where fruit is growing under the surface and to spot the signs of life approaching. I will trust you.

DRAW NEAR

Draw near to God,
and he will draw near to you.

JAMES 4:8 ESV

When we draw near to God, he draws even nearer to us.
When we turn to him, we find he is already facing. He does
not turn a cold shoulder. He never turns to leave. He is so
much closer than we realize, so let's turn our attention to
him. Let's open our hearts to his overwhelming love once
again.

Every morning is a fresh start. Every moment is a new
opportunity to seize. No matter where we are or what we
are struggling with today, Jesus is the open door to the
throne room of the Father. He is ever so near, and he is
ready to hear us, speak to us, and fill us with all we need.
Let's press into fellowship with our wonderful Creator God
today and be encouraged in his lifegiving love.

*Jesus, I draw near to you right now. I take time to turn my
attention to your presence. Please, draw even closer as
I do. Overwhelm my senses with your perfect peace and
speak to my heart. I am listening.*

CONFIDENT TRUST

Blessed is the one who trusts in the LORD,
whose confidence is in him.

JEREMIAH 17:7 NIV

The psalmist says to the Lord, "It is so much better to trust in you to save me than to put my confidence in someone else" (Psalm 118:8, TPT). Though we may have trustworthy allies and friends in our lives, none is more faithful than the Lord. He is always for his people.

What area of your life is stretching your faith? Is there something you need to break through that you cannot achieve on your own? It is good to find help in humanity, but it is even better to know your true confidence is in the Lord. May your heart be encouraged in his help and strength today.

Jesus, thank you for your faithful love toward your people. I trust you to continue to lead me into your goodness and work your miraculous mercy through the details of my life. Redeem what I cannot. Restore what I could only dream of. I trust you.

FULFILLED HOPES

Oh that I might have my request,
and that God would fulfill my hope.

JOB 6:8 ESV

Today, may you embrace the opportunity to lay out all your hopes before the Lord. He is near, he is listening, and he welcomes your honest pleas. Don't hold back any request. Jesus encouraged his disciples to ask in faith without holding back. May you seize the freedom and confidence that is yours to pour out your heart to him.

Proverbs 13:12 says, "Hope deferred makes the heart sick, but a desire fulfilled is a tree of life." Whatever your hopes, may you find strength to persevere in the waiting. There is more than enough grace. There is fullness of love, peace, and joy. When God fulfills your desires, may you know the all-surpassing satisfaction that is always yours in the liberty of fellowship with his Spirit.

Jesus, I rejoice when you answer my prayers, and I have learned to rejoice in the waiting. I know there is purpose here. Still, I won't suppress or deny the desires of my heart. Here's my heart, Lord; meet me with the reality of your presence and lead me in your wisdom.

THE LORD IS

The Lord is always good and ready to receive you.
He's so loving that it will amaze you—
so kind that it will astound you!
And he is famous for his faithfulness toward all.
Everyone knows our God can be trusted,
for he keeps his promises to every generation!

PSALM 100:5 TPT

The Lord is always good and ready to receive you. What an encouraging word that is for the day! We could camp on that sentence alone. We can repeat it and let it sink in until our shame dissipates, and we come with the confidence of dearly loved children before him. The good news is that this passage only gets better.

He's so loving that it will amaze you. Have you ever been amazed by someone's love toward you? *He's so kind that it will astound you!* His kindness will lead you to his presence every time. He is gentle toward you, offering you whatever it is that you need. His correction is not full of malice but of compassion. May you know the incomparable goodness of receiving his overwhelmingly loyal love in fresh ways today.

Jesus, thank you for the glorious goodness of your love. I don't want to miss a single truth you speak because I am distracted by the lies of shame and fear. Cover me with your peace, draw me in with kindness, and receive me with your delight.

GRACE ON GRACE

From his fullness we have all received,
grace upon grace.

JOHN 1:16 ESV

The life of Jesus was filled with grace. He was peace personified, the living image of love, and he taught about the abundant mercy of the Father. There are endless gifts of grace available to us whenever we need it. Not a drop will go to waste.

What do you need today? Are you exhausted? Do you need more focus? Do you require wisdom for decisions in front of you? Whatever it is, there is grace upon grace available for you through friendship with Jesus. There is more than enough for your needs in fellowship and companionship with his Spirit. Lean in and receive the grace he is offering you. He always knows just what you need, and he is not stingy.

Jesus, thank you for the gracious gift of your friendship and help. Thank you for saving me from the bondage of sin, shame, fear, and death. You are my wise leader and my friend. I rely on you for the help I need today and every day.

GREATER REWARD

"Love your enemies, do good to them, and lend to them without expecting to get anything back. Then your reward will be great, and you will be children of the Most High, because he is kind to the ungrateful and wicked."

LUKE 6:35 NIV

Jesus' instruction to treat our enemies with love was, and is, countercultural. He did not advocate ignoring them or turning a cold shoulder. He didn't say that we should dehumanize them. Love is an act of resistance against our natural tendencies when it is directed toward those who have hurt, disrespected, and abused us. This is not to say we should allow them the same access to our lives as those we trust.

Still, love is an expansive act that flies in the face of fear. It chooses to bless rather than to curse. It instructs our hearts and attitudes. It is a defiant act to offer love, even just within our own hearts, to those who are ungrateful. Our reward is better than reciprocity; it is from God himself. He is kind, and when we choose kindness, we represent him well.

Jesus, I want to choose love even when it goes against every instinct I have. Transform me in your mercy so I may choose kindness ever more readily. You are worthy of my surrender to love, and you are my great reward.

LIKE A CHILD

"Listen to the truth I speak: Whoever does not open their arms to receive God's kingdom like a teachable child will never enter it."

MARK 10:15 TPT

As we grow in understanding, let us never become so proud or arrogant that we think we know everything there is to know. We always know simply in part. Our understanding can constantly grow. We are conditioned in our cultures, families, and traditions; not everything we've known is based in the truth of God's kingdom. The pride of knowing better can keep us from the freedom of God's better ways if we're not careful. Let us remain humble in heart and open to seeing from a different perspective.

When we open our arms to receive God's kingdom like teachable children, we allow the Spirit of wisdom to instruct, correct, and guide us in love. Love makes room for all; it does not restrict who can come. It does not demand perfection. It does not expect full understanding. May love lead us into the wisdom of God's perspective.

Jesus, I want to be like a teachable child when it comes to your kingdom. I know I'm not done learning about you and how great your love is. Expand my understanding today as I open my heart to your leading and instruction.

RIGHTEOUS CHARACTER

May you always be filled with the fruit of your salvation—the righteous character produced in your life by Jesus Christ—for this will bring much glory and praise to God.

PHILIPPIANS 1:11 NLT

The fruit of our salvation is found in righteous character. Where does this righteousness come from? It comes from Christ. He is our covering, and our salvation is his gracious gift that no one can add to or take from.

Earlier in this chapter, Paul says that he prays that our love will overflow more and more because he wants us to understand what really matters. Righteous character is produced in loving relationship with Jesus Christ and in choosing to live with love as our banner, aim, and foundation. There is an abundance of love in Christ; it's a never-ending well that rises up until we overflow. God's love and righteousness go hand in hand.

Jesus, thank you for the gift of salvation through you. I am overwhelmed by the love you continue to pour out in ceaseless measure. Increase my love so that my life and choices will reflect your mercy and kindness more and more. You are my righteousness.

WHAT IS AHEAD

Let your eyes look straight ahead;
fix your gaze directly before you.

PROVERBS 4:25 NIV

When we spend time ruminating on the past, we allow the voices of regret, shame, and disappointment to take over. When we spend too much time looking into the future, we either get caught up in the fantasy of a better day or the anxiety of the unknown. Instead of looking too far behind or too far forward, let's take today as it is.

What is right in front of you today? What tasks are yours to do? What relationships need tending? What mundane chore is yours to tackle? You need not get ahead of yourself. Simply take the next step, and after you've done that, the next one after that. *Let your eyes look straight ahead; fix your gaze directly before you.*

Jesus, thank you for the reminder that this is the day you have made. I want to be mindfully aware and engaged in my relationships and what I'm doing today. Help me to focus and refocus on the here and now whenever I get overwhelmed.

RESTORED IN REFUGE

Keep me safe, my God,
for in you I take refuge.

PSALM 16:1 NIV

God is a safe harbor when the storms of life are raging. He is a place of refuge when enemies threaten us. We are the temple of the living God; Jesus said so. Those who are surrendered to the Lord are his living temples where his presence resides. We are never without his help because we are never without his presence.

May we find peace and restorative rest in his presence today. When the burdens of life are too much to bear, let's take respite in him. There is relief in the confidence of his faithfulness. There is so much room in his kindness to be human: to learn, to mess up, and to try again. He is our ultimate safe place, and he will never misuse or abuse us.

Jesus, you are better than any other. You are kinder, gentler, steadier, more understanding, and more powerful than any human I have ever known. I take refuge in you. Keep me safe, steady my heart, and love me to life again.

SUCCESSFUL PLANS

Commit your actions to the LORD,
and your plans will succeed.

PROVERBS 16:3 NLT

When we put our trust totally in God, not in the validity of our own ideas or our ability to make them happen, we leave room for God to work out our plans as he will. Our plans will succeed when we couple them with hard work, though little happens as we imagine it will. Even when we make plans, there will be subtle differences in the reality that we could not have foreseen in the planning stages.

God is a master builder. He is a creative artist. He knows how to work things together in beautifully mysterious ways. Through consistency, we build. Through endurance, we cultivate. We cannot put work in one day and then neglect it for the rest and expect to have anything. May we trust the Lord with our plans, and all the while put in the consistent effort it takes to move toward them.

Jesus, I love how you weave the threads of my life together into the tapestry of your mercy. As I step out into action on plans that have been laid out, I give you the reins. I trust you to do immeasurably more than I could with my yes and follow-through.

DON'T BE OFFENDED

"Blessed is anyone
who takes no offense at me."

MATTHEW 11:6 NRSV

Offense is easily found these days. It seems like every opinion is a hard-fought truth, but that is not the case. Do we allow room for love to correct us? Does compassion have space to move us outside our own perspective?

We have biases, and we have strong values. When those are interrupted or brought into question by another, we have a choice to make. Will we let offense build a wall around us, or will we listen with an openness to understand where the other is coming from even if we remain in disagreement? Only we can choose how we will react. Above all, let's stay open to the ways and teachings of Jesus Christ. He never fails.

Jesus, keep my heart humble. I don't want to be too proud to hear another point of view or an opposing reality from my own experience. I am open to your mercy, and I know that means I get to choose your mercy in my relationships with others. Help me to remain resolute in your love above all else.

EVERY MORNING

Lord, every morning you hear my voice.
Every morning, I tell you what I need,
and I wait for your answer.

PSALM 5:3 NCV

Today's verse is a glorious reminder that the Lord is available right now. He is listening. He is ready. He is full of compassion and full of wisdom. It doesn't matter how long or short a time it's been since we turned our attention to him; he is already turned toward us.

Take time to regulate your heart in the love of Christ. Pour out your heart and mind. Talk to him. Don't hold anything back. Tell him what it is you need and make a practice of waiting on his answer. Be honest and open. Listen. He is always ready to meet you. He is always listening.

Jesus, thank you for the open reception I have in your presence. Thank you for meeting me with your limitless mercy every time I come to you. I won't stop turning toward you, for you are life and breath and peace and joy. You are the sun, and I turn my face toward you.

EVERY DETAIL

We are convinced that every detail of our lives is continually woven together to fit into God's perfect plan of bringing good into our lives, for we are his lovers who have been called to fulfill his designed purpose.

ROMANS 8:28 TPT

Even areas we see as useless in our lives are woven into the fabric of God's great mercy. He doesn't miss even the smallest opportunity to bring beauty out of ashes. His redemptive power is at work in the details as much as it is in the overarching themes of our lives.

May you find encouragement in the restorative love of Jesus Christ today. May you find your confidence rooted in his nature more than your own. His faithful mercy never misses the mark. May you find your purpose in being his and in pursuing what he has put in your heart to pursue. His goodness is with you always.

Jesus, thank you for the many ways you weave your goodness into the minutiae of my story. I believe you will continue to treat me with kindness. I don't need to worry about how everything will fit together. You are trustworthy, and I am confident in your character.

HIS GOODNESS CONTINUES

I am certain that God, who began the good work within you, will continue his work until it is finally finished on the day when Christ Jesus returns.

PHILIPPIANS 1:6 NLT

Wherever this finds you today, may you not lose hope in the redemptive mercy of God. His power is at work in the details of your life, and he will not let anything go to waste. When you grieve, you do not grieve without hope. The sun will rise again, and you will surely experience the overwhelming delight of his goodness in your life once again.

Jesus continues to do his work today. He has not let up in love, and he has not withheld his kindness from you. He is as near as he ever was. Lean into his Spirit and find rest in his presence. There is more to life, and there is more that he is doing in and around you.

Jesus, thank you for never giving up. Even when I struggle to hope, you do not waver in your overwhelming love, not even a little! Give me eyes to see, ears to hear, and a heart that understands your perspective. Complete your good work in me.

MUCH MORE VALUABLE

"Look at all the birds—do you think they worry about
their existence? They don't plant or reap or store up
food, yet your heavenly Father provides them each with
food. Aren't you much more valuable to your Father
than they?"

MATTHEW 6:26 TPT

When we live with hearts of trust surrendered to the
Father, there is no need to worry about the necessities of
life. In this passage, Jesus encouraged his followers in the
same way the Father instructed his people to not be afraid.
Just as the old Scriptures encouraged readers in God's
faithfulness, so did Jesus.

Where there is worry about the future, let's turn to Jesus
in trust. Where there is anxiety about the unknowns ahead,
may we let go of the need to control and allow the peace
of God that transcends understanding lay hold of our
hearts through his Spirit. The Father has not changed.
Jesus remains the same, and the Spirit is here to remind us
of his loyal love. May we release our grip in loving trust and
refocus on what remains true in him.

*Jesus, I give you my worry and anxiety. I don't want to
carry their weight. Fill me with your peace and wisdom,
and let my focus be clearly fixed on you and your kingdom
purposes.*

UNENDING BLESSINGS

Surely you have granted him unending blessings
and made him glad with the joy of your presence.

PSALM 21:6 NIV

David penned the beginning of this psalm of praise while
looking back over experiences he had with the Lord. We
can turn our experiences into praise as well with the gift of
hindsight. Where have you seen God come through for you in
faithfulness? Where has he deposited blessings in your life?

You are living in the outpouring of his love. Even when
you walk through valleys where it is hard to see and the
shadows grow long, his mercy is with you as you journey.
May you take the opportunity to look back over your walk
with the Lord and be encouraged where you find answers
to prayer, the incomparable goodness of his presence with
you, and the promise of his continued faithfulness.

*Jesus, as I look over my history with you, will you
encourage my heart in your faithfulness? I believe
you aren't finished with me yet. Fill me with hopeful
expectation for what is to come even as I rejoice in what
you have already done.*

PROVEN PASSION

Christ proved God's passionate love for us by dying in our place while we were still lost and ungodly!

ROMANS 5:8 TPT

The passion of Christ sent him not only to the earth to be clothed in humanity, but also to the cross where he was put to death for us. Jesus did not need to die in order for us to know God's love, and yet the love of God knew no bounds.

There is no greater love than this: that a person would lay down their life for their friends. These were Jesus' words in John 15. Jesus did even more than this. He laid down his life, not just for his friends at the time, but for all who would ever come to him. What a beautiful Savior! What a wonderful love. Where there has been doubt of the power of Christ's love, may there be renewed understanding and fresh perspective of his mercy.

Jesus, thank you for paying the ultimate price so that I could know you and so that everyone who looks to you might be saved. I am humbled by your love again. You are better than anyone I have ever known.

BREAD OF PEACE

It is in vain that you rise up early and go late to rest,
eating the bread of anxious toil;
for he gives to his beloved sleep.

Psalm 127:2 esv

How much of your day is driven by anxiety? How much is
fueled by rest? When we are going on overdrive, we will hit
a wall at some point. We cannot control what we will come
up against throughout our day, but we certainly can trust
that God's grace will meet us in every circumstance.

Instead of swirling in the current of what we cannot
control, let's carve out times of rejuvenation and play. Let's
not forget to create rhythms of rest where we step off the
hamster wheel of have-to into the space of get-to. A well-
balanced life is a life that can be enjoyed in both work and
recreation. Let's value our rest as much as we do our work,
for we are always worthy of love no matter what we're
doing or not doing.

*Jesus, I want to learn how to be as present in leisure as I
am in work. I don't want to overvalue my productivity and
neglect my well-being. Teach me how to balance this in
your love.*

HEART FLOW

Above all else, guard your heart,
for everything you do flows from it.

PROVERBS 4:23 NIV

Our hearts are not only the place where we feel affection; it also includes our thoughts, will, and discernment. It is in this place, our innermost being, where we live. Our actions do not appear from thin air. They reflect our core beliefs, our experiences, and our conditioning.

How much care do you give your heart? How much attention do you pay to your thoughts, will, and discernment? Not everything we think is true. That is important to recognize. If we can approach our thoughts with curiosity rather than judgment, we can open ourselves to other possibilities and the voice of wisdom.

Jesus, I want my heart to align with your kingdom values. Thank you for the gift of your wisdom to guide, instruct, heal, and correct me. I lean into you, and I trust your love to meet me in every space—including in my heart.

PEACE PROMISES

"I have told you all this so that you may have peace in me. Here on earth you will have many trials and sorrows. But take heart, because I have overcome the world."

JOHN 16:33 NLT

The makeup of our lives (the circumstances, victories, and trials) is not a reflection of the favor of God. Though his mercy is evident in his faithfulness toward us, we cannot measure our worth according to the level of ease or difficulty we face.

Jesus told his followers they would face many trials and walk through many sorrows. This remains true today. Still, he promised that we would find, and keep, peace in him through it all. His peace is our portion today and forever. May we take heart and take hope in Christ's promises, for he has overcome the world. That includes all our fears!

Jesus, you are the Prince of Peace. Meet me with the overwhelming goodness of your nearness in your presence today. Spirit, draw near and encourage me with your love. Thank you for your unending mercy that never changes toward me no matter what I'm going through.

MORE TO LEARN

"Call to me and I will answer you, and will tell you great and hidden things that you have not known."

JEREMIAH 33:3 ESV

We can never reach the end of knowing God. We have not even scratched the surface of his wisdom's ways. He is full of perfect perspective, unshakeable love, unflinching power, and unyielding grace. There are great and hidden things we can discover in him, and there is always more to uncover.

Let's call on him and wait for his answer. As we do, he will reveal things remained hidden to us before. He will unlock the mysteries of his kingdom and offer solutions only he could know. When we rely on him as teacher and advisor, we make room for his voice to instruct us in better ways than we could come up with on our own.

Jesus, thank you for your invitation to call to you at all times. I come to you yet again with a heart that is hungry to know you. Reveal yourself to me in fresh ways and give me revelations of your goodness. Thank you.

JULY

This is the day that the Lord has made;
let us rejoice and be glad in it.

PSALM 118:24 NRSV

WORDS THAT LIFT

Anxiety weighs down the heart,
but a kind word cheers it up.

PROVERBS 12:25 NIV

Can there be a kinder word than the everlasting joy we have found in Christ? He is full of life, hope, salvation, joy, all we long for, and so much more than we can imagine. Though anxiety is a real struggle, especially on overwhelming days, there is a greater hope still alive in Jesus.

When our hearts are heavy with worry, let's turn to the Lord. When they are sick with dread, let's turn our attention to his steadfast love. He is faithful. He is true. He is full of justice and power. He will not fail. He is still God. He is still good. Let's fill our minds with the truth, and let's look to encourage each other in Christ as long as it is called today.

Jesus, speak your words of life over my heart, mind, and body. Fill me with the knowledge of your goodness that knows no bounds. Lift the heavy weight of worry off my back as I yield my thoughts to you again.

FOREVER PORTION

My flesh and my heart may fail,
but God is the strength of my heart
and my portion forever.

PSALM 73:26 NIV

When our bodies fail us, God remains steadfast and strong in love. When our hearts lose hope, the faithfulness of God is immoveable. No matter what we feel or experience, God is still good. He is still real. He is still powerful. He is still accessible through Christ.

May the Spirit of Christ strengthen your heart in his pools of refreshing love today. May his plentiful portion of peace nourish your body. May you find all you need in the abundance of his presence as it washes over you. His love never grows stale. It is dense with nutrients, and it is fuel for whatever we face. He is more than enough, and he always will be.

Jesus, you are my forever portion, my abundance, and my strength. Fill me with the fruit of your Spirit today and wash over me with your living waters. You are my sustenance, and I need you more than anything else.

NO SEPARATION

I am convinced that nothing can ever separate us from God's love. Neither death nor life, neither angels nor demons, neither our fears for today nor our worries about tomorrow—not even the powers of hell can separate us from God's love.

ROMANS 8:38 NLT

If you find yourself with extra time this morning, evening, or any space between, spend some time in this chapter of Romans. It is filled with wisdom about living by the power of the Holy Spirit, our identities as daughters of the living God, and the glorious destiny that awaits us in his kingdom.

The triumph of God's love is on full display for all to see, hear, taste, and repeat. There is absolutely nothing that can separate us from God's love. What a glorious message this is! Nothing real or imagined, fraught with fear or filled with enticement, can keep us from the overwhelming goodness of the power of Christ's love. Nothing. No one. Nowhere. Love is abundant, and it is present today and forever.

Jesus, thank you for the incomparable power of your love that cannot be diminished or disregarded. Your love is greater than anything else, and I trust in its power in my life. Thank you for this wisdom.

EVERY DAY OF MY LIFE

Surely your goodness and love
will follow me all the days of my life,
and I will dwell in the house of the Lord forever.

PSALM 23:6 NIV

When you are faced with worries about the future, may
you find respite in the truth of God's Word. His promised
love never leaves you. His goodness will never let up. He is
faithful, and he cannot change. Once promised, he follows
through. Once spoken, he backs up his words with loyal love.

Take a few moments today to speak this verse aloud.
Proclaim it over your day. Prophesy it over your life. If you
are in Christ, then you are his. You belong to him. Surely his
goodness and love will follow you all the days of your life.
You will dwell in the house of the Lord forever! Amen.

*Jesus, thank you for your goodness and love that follow
me. Your mercy always reaches me. Your kindness always
follows me. I yield my heart, my life, my attention, and my
intentions to you. Fill my mind with your peace as I speak
your Word over my heart.*

COMFORT AND STRENGTH

Your words have comforted those who fell,
and you have strengthened those who could not stand.

JOB 4:4 NCV

Have you ever been comforted by the Lord in a moment of complete failure or weakness? Have you experienced the strength of God through his Spirit when grief had gained hold of your heart? If you cannot think of a moment where the Spirit of God was both comfort and strength to you in hard times, may you find yourself held and empowered by him now.

Every moment is an opportunity to experience the fullness of his love. Every situation, no matter how wonderful or dire, is full of access to his presence. May you know his peace that passes all understanding, the comfort of his wrap-around presence, and the relief of his joy.

Jesus, be my comfort in sorrow and my strength in weakness. I don't want to just know about you; I want to know you. As real as my friends and family are, be real to me. As close as my closest friend, draw near to me. I want more, Lord.

COME WITH CONFIDENCE

"If you can?" said Jesus.
"Everything is possible
for one who believes."

MARK 9:23 NIV

May you find courage rather than condemnation in the words of Jesus today. When you pray, he hears and welcomes you. When you ask, don't ask like a beggar but as a child. When you make your request, there's no need to wonder if he's able. He can do all things.

Jesus is quick to respond in mercy, so don't hold back your requests from him. Come with confidence and not wavering in worry or doubt. Even if you did, he would meet you. However, the more you get to know him, the more transformed you will be by his faithful love. Let that be your foundation and your confidence. Come with boldness before the throne of your Maker!

Jesus, I will pray with confidence and make all my requests with faith in your ability to do far more than I could even think to ask. You are better than I am, and I believe that you hear me, answer me, and are infinitely good. I trust you.

VERY GOOD

God looked over all he had made,
and he saw that it was very good!

GENESIS 1:31 NLT

You were made in the image of God. You, with all your perceived flaws and faults, were made with intention and creativity to reflect his image. You are not an afterthought or mistake. You are wonderfully made!

When you read the verse for today, remember that you are included in all God made. He looked over creation after that first week and declared that it was good. When he creates, he makes no mistakes. Will you let the confidence of his love wash over your heart as you remember that you reflect his goodness? You certainly are.

Jesus, thank you for making me with love and intention. I will not despise what you have said is good. I will not tear down what you have declared worthy of your love. I have found fullness of life, love, peace, joy, and acceptance in you. Thank you.

MORE MERCY

Let us then approach God's throne of grace with confidence, so that we may receive mercy and find grace to help us in our time of need.

HEBREWS 4:16 NIV

In your time of need, there is no reason to despair. When you have reached the end of your rope, grab hold of Christ's, for it is never-ending. He has more than enough love to empower you, grace to strengthen you, and hope to encourage you.

Approach the throne of your Father with confidence today in the knowledge you are seen, heard, welcomed, and accepted. There, you will find the grace you need to help you face whatever comes your way today. Don't jump too far ahead; let today's challenges be enough. Christ is your unending portion, and he is with you here and now. Take it one step at a time, and never stop coming to him for more mercy and grace whenever you need it.

Jesus, you are my source of power, hope, and courage. You are my life source. Fill me up with what I need for today as I spend time in your presence. Walk with me, for I rely on your help.

RENEWED STRENGTH

Those who hope in the LORD will renew their strength.
They will soar on wings like eagles;
they will run and not grow weary,
they will walk and not be faint.

ISAIAH 40:31 NIV

Every need is an opportunity to be met by the Lord. When we run out of strength, there is a storehouse of grace in the kingdom of our God. When we are weary, we rely on God's strength to lift us up and empower us.

We all know the weariness that comes with living in this world. It cannot be avoided. Still, this passage is a beautiful reminder that when we put our hope in the Lord, we trust him to take care of what we cannot on our own. We will soar on wings like eagles. We will run and not grow weary; we will walk and not be faint. In his Spirit, we experience renewal over and over again. Let's lean into his life within us when our own is waning.

Jesus, the fact is that I am tired. I am weary. I rely on your grace to meet me and renew my strength. Be everything I need and empower me to keep persevering in your Spirit. Please, give me rest in the midst of it all.

PURE WISDOM

The wisdom that comes from God is first of all pure, then peaceful, gentle, and easy to please. This wisdom is always ready to help those who are troubled and to do good for others. It is always fair and honest.

JAMES 3:17 NCV

The wisdom of God is easily found in Christ. It is in everything he did, said, and in the fruits of his Spirit. He remains steadfast in loving truth; he hasn't changed a bit. The wisdom of Christ is often simple, not complex. It is not a ten-step plan. It is often just the next step, but that is all we need.

May we not despise the simplicity of Christ's commands, and may we not lose sight of the power of his love. He is not a demanding master but a faithful friend. He will not degrade us in our failures. He lifts us up and encourages us with his grace when we are weak. The more we get to know Jesus, the more readily we will discern his wisdom.

Jesus, thank you for the simplicity of your wisdom that does not require more than I am able to offer. Speak to me and guide me in your loving truth today. I rely on you.

FRUIT OF PATIENCE

A person's wisdom yields patience;
it is to one's glory to overlook an offense.

PROVERBS 19:11 NIV

Patience does not come easily to many of us. This is especially in this instant age where we can have almost anything we can think of with a couple clicks of a button. May we not despise the process of waiting, for there is so much outside of our control that we cannot force to come more quickly.

Maybe your parent often repeated the phrase "patience is a virtue" when you were a child. You wanted to move faster and get to the exciting parts of your day. And though the phrase may sound rote, there is benefit in cultivating a patient heart. When we let go of our need to control, we can take hold of God's wisdom instead. We cannot avoid the waiting periods of life, but we can learn to lean into them and to find beauty in the process.

Jesus, I don't want to confuse patience for indifference, and I never want to seek control over another because of my discomfort with waiting. Help me to find the messy middle where you meet me in the waiting. I trust you more than I trust myself.

EVEN THEN

Even when I walk through the darkest valley,
I will not be afraid, for you are close beside me.
Your rod and your staff protect and comfort me.

PSALM 23:4 NLT

There will come a time in your life when you walk through a dark valley. It is unavoidable. Grief closes in on the heels of loss. Depression may sink into your heart. You may experience a life-altering sickness or diagnosis. You need to know that even in the darkest valley, Christ is close beside you.

Even when it seems your world has turned upside down, God has not left you. He is near. He is a shepherd, and he keeps track of his sheep. You are his daughter, and he will not let you out of his sight. He will continue to protect and comfort you. His Spirit surrounds you. Lean in, turn your awareness toward him, and be held.

Jesus, I trust that when nothing makes sense in my life, you have not changed. You still know the end from the beginning. I will not let fear overtake me, for you are my Shepherd, my faithful friend, and my comfort. Please, stay close!

WAY MAKER

Seek his will in all you do,
and he will show you which path to take.

PROVERBS 3:6 NLT

When you look to the Lord for guidance and help, you can be sure he will not let you wander from his love. He will show you where to walk when you have no idea what to do. When you seek his wise counsel, he will freely give it to you.

When you cannot discern which way to go, lean in to hear his voice. What is he saying? Does your heart pull one way over another? Do you feel the freedom to choose what you will and the confidence that God will redirect you if need be? His will is not a tightrope that only the highly trained can walk. He is so much larger than that. Trust that he will guide you with the tide of his love.

Jesus, I am so grateful that your love is larger than my miniscule understanding of it. I trust that when I look to you for help, I have it. Even as I walk forward, I know you go with me, and you will redirect me in kindness when needed.

RISE UP IN COURAGE

Lord, you are my shield,
my wonderful God who gives me courage.

PSALM 3:3 NCV

Jesus Christ is our shield and our protection. We have been wrapped up into him and covered by his love in the eyes of the Father. We are clothed in the mercy of Christ that covers all our sin and shame. What a wonderful gift to be pure and free in his love!

Knowing this, we can rise up in courage to face whatever comes. There is no shame that can claim us as its own. Fear's voice is not our master. The merciful kindness of God, his saving grace and powerful resurrection, is our covering. Why would we be afraid of anything when God has completely liberated us in his love?

Jesus, your mercy is my courage and my strength. Thank you for the freedom I have in you. I am able to face head-on whatever comes my way because you are with me, and you have declared me liberated and whole in your love.

FREE FROM WORRY

"Remain passionate and free from anxiety and the worries of this life. Then you will not be caught off guard by what happens."

LUKE 21:34 TPT

When we remain in the love of God instead of letting our hearts grow cold, we actively cultivate the passion of his compassion within our lives. Where there is apathy, a coldness has crept in. May we be diligent in looking at our own indifference to others with curiosity. May we not lose sight of our shared humanity.

The worries of this life have a way of creeping in and taking over our mental load. If we are not careful, they will redirect our hearts and drain our emotional capacity. May we lay down our worries with Jesus and only taking back what we can do. We are not responsible for mastering the unknown. We cannot know the future, but we know the one who does. May we trust him with what we cannot control.

Jesus, I want to live free from the weight of worry. Teach me to let go of that which is not mine to carry. Help me remain strong in your love and burn through the cold apathy that can build up in this world. I trust you.

SPIRIT OF TRUTH

"When the Spirit of truth comes, he will guide you into all truth. He will not speak on his own but will tell you what he has heard."

JOHN 16:13 NLT

The Spirit of truth is not found in some far-off land that we need to journey to. It is not found by lashes or by sword. It is not something to overtake or control. The Spirit of truth is the Spirit of God himself. It is the Holy Spirit.

Have you ever felt like truth is only found within the walls of a church or on the lips of a preacher? The Spirit of God is not confined to buildings or to people with certain titles. The Spirit of truth is as much with you as he is with any other. You have access to the wisdom, grace, and mercy of God through the Spirit of God with you. Don't buy into anyone's power play to control you. The truth is not controlling; it sets you free.

Jesus, thank you for the liberty of your mercy and for the accessibility of your wise truth through fellowship with your Spirit. I'm so grateful I don't need to search under rocks or travel to cathedrals to find you, know you, and be taught by you.

NEVER-ENDING LOVE

"For the mountains may depart
and the hills be removed,
but my steadfast love shall not depart from you,
and my covenant of peace shall not be removed,"
says the LORD, who has compassion on you.

ISAIAH 54:10 ESV

The world has seen many wars. It has known plague and famine. Everything we experience has been experienced before. May we not give into despair, for God's love is powerful to save. He will see us through our trials and our challenges. Civilizations rise and fall; that is the way of the world. When we see our own begin to crumble, may we remember that God is bigger than a nation. He is more steadfast than any government.

May you be drenched in the living love of God's presence today as you look to him. May hope rise within your heart and break through the soil of disappointment. We cannot have one without the other. God is a master at redeeming what seemed forever lost and bringing new life out of the ashes.

Jesus, you are my peace, my courage, and my strength. I want to see from your perspective today. Give me a glimpse of the largeness of eternity's view and breathe hope into my feeble heart.

HOLY MOTIVATIONS

Let us think of ways to motivate one another
to acts of love and good works.

HEBREWS 10:24 NLT

What would our communities look like if we took these
words to heart? What if we tried to outdo one another in
love and goodness? We know how to compete already;
why not compete to be the bigger blessing?

How can you help others motivate one another in love? It
is as simple as starting with you. What can you do to show
practical care to someone in your community? What good
work is obvious and yet has not been taken up by anyone
else? It doesn't have to be big to matter. Even the smallest
acts of kindness can be a huge boost to the one in need of it.

Jesus, I love this thought! I want to be creative in loving
others in practical ways. Will you give me the insight and
creativity to show up and serve others in love in both little
and large ways?

CALLED TO FREEDOM

You have been called to live in freedom, my brothers and sisters. But don't use your freedom to satisfy your sinful nature. Instead, use your freedom to serve one another in love.

GALATIANS 5:13 NLT

Many of us know the benefits of freedom. We probably have a good handle on what our idea of freedom looks like. The details may be different, depending on where we make our homes and what our values are. No matter where we are from, we should keep in mind that our freedom should be used to show love to others instead of in self-service.

Jesus was free to do as he pleased, yet he used his freedom to serve others and show them the love of the Father. Our lives will look different from his, but may our heart motivations, along with our actions, align with his values. Let's use the liberty we have been given to serve others in love and not just to build safe spaces of comfort for ourselves.

Jesus, I want my life to reflect your love in all I do and in the freedoms I choose to uphold. Show me how to lay down my own rights to serve the greater good and your kingdom.

GIFT OF GOD

By grace you have been saved through faith.
And this is not your own doing; it is the gift of God.

EPHESIANS 2:8 ESV

The grace of God is a glorious gift. Nothing we do can garner us more favor with him. Nothing we say can take away from the power of his salvation. When we align our lives in his mercy, his fruit will speak for itself. However, God is not after us for what we can offer him. He does not pursue us so that we will do things for him.

In loving relationship, we are whole. By grace, we have been saved through faith. Nothing we have done even makes a dent in that grace. May we live our lives knowing Christ and being known by him in living relationship. It is an offering that only he could give to us, and we are all recipients of the same abundantly good gift.

Jesus, I stop my striving today and give up my need to earn your favor. I am grateful that I already have it by your grace. Thank you! I am humbled by your love, and I am encouraged to share your love with others. I know you offer it to all in the same measure.

RIVER OF JUSTICE

Let justice flow like a river,
and let goodness flow like a never-ending stream.

AMOS 5:24 NCV

When we choose to turn our eyes from justice, our lives are empty shells and our praises like clanging symbols that make noise to cover the voices of others. When we know there are people suffering under the weight of injustice and we choose to ignore it, we are not living the embodied mercy of Christ.

May our lives be directed by the goodness of God. May we offer shelter to those who are misplaced and a listening ear to those who have suffered. Let's offer bedding and food and comfort to those who are weary from their war-torn lands. Let's join with the vulnerable and lift them up. Let's put our resources where our mouths are, and let's not lose sight of God's mercy toward all.

Jesus, I want to live with more intention than I have been. I want to walk the walk of advocating for those who are vulnerable. I have so much, and I will look for ways to serve those who are suffering with what I can offer. Thank you for this practical reminder.

NO MATTER WHAT

Each time he said, "My grace is all you need.
My power works best in weakness."
So now I am glad to boast about my weaknesses,
so that the power of Christ can work through me.

2 CORINTHIANS 12:9 NLT

The vivacity of kingdom of God is not dependent on our strength. It doesn't need our power to be victorious. As children of God, we are citizens of Christ's kingdom above all else. His kingdom ways and values become our own. We have free and full access to Jesus' grace at all times. His power works best in our weakness because that's when we rely on him most.

May you treat every weakness and failure as an opportunity for God to fill in and show off his restorative mercy. He can do far more with a willing heart than a proud one. May you lean into his strength and find encouragement today.

Jesus, you use the weak and foolish things of this world to shame the proud and those who are wise in their own eyes. I want to be found in you and reliant on your grace. Cover my weakness, Lord. Show everyone your power.

GREATER THAN FEAR

God will never give you the spirit of fear,
but the Holy Spirit who gives you mighty power,
love, and self-control.

1 TIMOTHY 1:7 TPT

When fear is in the driver's seat of our minds, hearts, or lives, we can be sure that God is not moving us. This is not to shame anyone for the times when fear has taken over. Not by any means! Fear is both a stress and trauma response. Even so, let us not mistake fear for God's leading.

There is space in the wisdom of God. There is love in his leading. There is mighty power to do more than we could on our own. There is self-control to move at a reasonable and right pace. Let's not stay stuck or rush ahead in fear. Let's invite the leadership of God through the Holy Spirit to strengthen, guide, and help us in all things.

Jesus, I know you don't barter in fear, and you don't require blind obedience. I won't be afraid to give you my honest concerns and hesitations, and I will let your love draw me to you once again. Please, settle your peace into my heart.

ANSWERED

When I was in trouble, I called to the LORD,
and he answered me.

PSALM 120:1 NCV

Beloved, it does not matter how small, how big, how
complex, or how simple your troubles are; God will help
you with them all. Don't hold back your prayers or requests
from him. Don't hesitate to call on him in everything. He is
a loving father and a willing help.

In Joel, God spoke through the prophet and said, "Anyone
who calls on the Lord will be saved." Anyone who calls on
the name of Jesus Christ will be answered and saved. This
is God's truth. Call on him with confidence not only for
your soul but also for your circumstances. He is a ready
and strong advocate who will rise up on your behalf.

*Jesus, thank you for the promise of your help when I call
on you. I won't hesitate to call on your name no matter the
circumstance. I rely on you more than any other. I won't
stop crying out to you, Lord.*

BLINK OF AN EYE

It will happen in a moment, in the blink of an eye, when the last trumpet is blown. For when the trumpet sounds, those who have died will be raised to live forever. And we who are living will also be transformed.

1 CORINTHIANS 15:52 NLT

Though the days may seem long, everything can change in a moment. Let's not lose sight of how quickly one change can pivot our entire lives. May we be full of grace, hope, and reverence. May we hold what we have loosely, and may we cherish the blessings in our lives.

The process of transformation is not quick or easy, but there are moments that shift everything. Let's look to the future with hope as the resurrection power of Jesus continues to move. He will fulfill every promise he has made. He will do everything he said he would. In the meantime, let's live with intention, love, and gracious, open hearts.

Jesus, you are the fullness of hope. In you, there will be fulfillment for every longing of the earth. You will come again, and when you do, you will set everything according to the laws of your kingdom. All that's wrong will be made right. Hallelujah!

UNENDING RIGHTEOUSNESS

In keeping with his promise we are looking
forward to a new heaven and a new earth,
where righteousness dwells.

2 PETER 3:13 NIV

When the world is too much to bear, when the weight of
the trauma and troubles gets heavier by the moment, may
you find rest in the presence of Jesus. He has not stopped
being God. He has not lost sight of anyone or anything.
He is still powerful in mercy. He is still the God of the
impossible. He is full of loyal love and saving grace.

Perhaps you can fix your eyes on the promise of his
kingdom coming. We catch glimpses of this glory through
his Spirit in our lives. We experience miracles of mercy. The
fullness of his kingdom and its perfection is still coming.
There is more, and it is good. It is better than we can
imagine, and so is he.

*Jesus, thank you for the reminder of your promises to
establish a new heaven and earth, to wipe every tear
from our eyes, and to bring perfect peace to that which is
chaos now. I trust you. Please, fill my heart with hope as I
look to you.*

PRAISE HIM

Let everything that breathes
praise the Lord.
Praise the Lord!

Psalm 150:6 ncv

With every breath we breathe, we have an opportunity to praise the Lord. It need not be with shouts or songs. It can be with quiet thanks and a heart of gratitude. It can be as simple as remembering you are seen and known by the Creator of all things. It can be as miniscule as a moment of acknowledgment of his presence with you.

Perhaps you do not feel grateful for much. Can you thank him for the air that fills your lungs in this moment? Can you thank him for the earth beneath you? The food in your belly? Whatever it is that nourishes and keeps you in this moment is an avenue of gratitude if you will let it.

Jesus, I praise you for the sun that filters through my window. I praise you for the breath that eases in and out of my lungs. I praise you for another day of life. For all this and more, I praise you.

EVEN STILL

If we are not faithful, he will still be faithful,
because he must be true to who he is.

2 TIMOTHY 2:13 NCV

The constancy of God's character, his very nature, is wonderful news for us. He is merciful because of the compelling nature of his love and not because of what we do or do not do. He is faithful because it is his nature to follow through on his Word. He does not depend on our faith or our follow-through. He is far above us.

Praise God that his faithfulness does not depend on our own. He does not need us, and yet he chooses to partner with us when we yield our hearts and lives to him. May our confidence in his loyal love increase with the realization that he is not tethered to or held back by our mistakes. His resurrection power brings life out of death every time.

Jesus, I am so grateful that your ways are higher than my own. I am forever humbled by your love. You do not need my yes to follow through on your promises, yet you honor my yes when I give it. Thank you.

MARINATE IN CHRIST'S TEACHING

Let the teaching of Christ live in you richly. Use all wisdom to teach and instruct each other by singing psalms, hymns, and spiritual songs with thankfulness in your hearts to God.

COLOSSIANS 3:16 NCV

The teachings of Christ are rich. They are full of lifegiving wisdom, power to overcome, and encouragement in the face of disappointment. Let's not forget the joy of his lessons. Paul's instruction to teach and instruct each other through song is an important reminder that spiritual music is holy.

What are your favorite songs of worship? Is there a hymn, psalm, or praise song that has stuck with you in this season? Spend some time listening to it. There is wisdom in the spoken word, the sung truth, and the inspiring chord. May your heart marinate in the truth of Christ's teaching as it is played through music that ministers to your spirit.

Jesus, I will sing a new song to you today. I will spend time listening to music that reflects your love, your wisdom, and your power. Thank you for the language of music that engages not just my mind but with my whole soul.

INNER STRENGTH

I pray that from his glorious, unlimited resources he will empower you with inner strength through his Spirit.

EPHESIANS 3:16 NLT

Paul prayed that the love of Christ would overflow in the readers of his letter. He prayed that the unlimited resources of Christ's kingdom would empower them with inner strength. He prayed for the power of God's Spirit to strengthen and encourage them.

As I write this, I pray the same over you. "I pray that from his glorious, unlimited resources he will empower you with inner strength through his Spirit." May you know the glorious hope of he who has called you his own. You are a part of the kingdom of God and a co-heir with Christ. May you be filled with all you need, and more than you can imagine, in fellowship with his Spirit. May you be blessed today.

Jesus, thank you for the power of prayer through all generations and ages. I know there is power in your Word, and I believe what has been proclaimed is mine to take hold of.

TENDERHEARTED FORGIVENESS

Be kind to each other, tenderhearted, forgiving one another, just as God through Christ has forgiven you.

EPHESIANS 4:32 NLT

When our hearts remain humble in Christ's love, we are able to choose forgiveness over the pride of our offenses. When we forgive, we release ourselves from holding on to the bitter roots of disappointment and accusation. Though healing takes time and accountability is important, we must learn to walk in all the ways of Jesus. One of the foremost ways is to walk in tenderhearted mercy.

We have been forgiven of all our faults, flaws, and failures in the great love of Christ. He holds nothing against us. What he refuses to hold against us, let us also not hold against ourselves or one another. Let's be quick to forgive; it makes room for the abundance of love to fill us even more.

Jesus, your love is my motivation in all things. With your mercy, empower me to let go of my unforgiveness. I know it does not serve me well. I trust you will show me how to forgive and how to honor you, others, and myself in that action.

AUGUST

Weeping may linger for the night,
but joy comes with the morning.

Psalm 30:5 nrsv

NOTHING IS HIDDEN

Nothing in all creation is hidden from God.
Everything is naked and exposed before his eyes,
and he is the one to whom we are accountable.

HEBREWS 4:13 NLT

We cannot hide anything from God. He sees everything clearly. He's not surprised by our biases or our habits. He knows us better than we know ourselves. However, this is not an excuse to continue in shame-based movements when we are aware of them. We are accountable to him. We cannot offend God, but we are still called to live in his love.

Is there an area of your life that does not align in his mercy? Is there something you have kept doing, thinking, or saying even though you know it doesn't reflect the kindness of his heart toward you or others? May you bring it to Jesus today. He is ready to meet you with kindness and truth.

Jesus, your wisdom is better than any excuse I have made. I believe you are kind, true, and full of redemptive power. I look to you. I come to you with the things I have tried to hide, and I ask for your mercy to meet me here and now.

WHEN YOU ARE TIRED

He gives strength to those who are tired
and more power to those who are weak.

ISAIAH 40:29 NCV

Take this as your invitation to find both strength and rest in Jesus today. When you are tired, he offers his own grace to strengthen you. When you are weak, he gives you his power. There is more than enough in his abundant storehouse. He never runs low, and he never runs out. Lean on him, and he will lift you up.

Perhaps you find yourself with energy to spare. If that's the case, perhaps it would be a good opportunity to lend a hand to someone in need. We reflect the goodness of God when we give generously from the overflow of our lives. Wherever you find yourself, whether on the receiving or the giving end today, may you be blessed with the generosity of God's power in your life.

Jesus, I lean on your strength when my own is depleted. Thank you for loving me the same whether I am weary or full of vitality. I partner with your heart today. Fill me up so that I am able to meet others' needs as well.

BE EMBRACED

"Everyone my Father has given to me, they will come. And all who come to me, I will embrace and will never turn them away."

JOHN 6:37 TPT

Jesus' arms are open to you. He has not changed his mind about you. The burdens or failures of yesterday have not convinced him to step back. He is as full of loyal love toward you now as he ever has been or ever will be.

You are a gift to Jesus. Come to him and be embraced. He will never turn you away. He won't abandon you in your need. He won't scold you or abuse you. He is tenderhearted and overflowing with mercy that heals, restores, and redeems. Don't let anything hold you back today; come to him with all your shame, all your fears, and all your questions. Come and be embraced!

Jesus, thank you for welcoming me with open arms of love. I won't stay away, and I won't give in to shame's fear of being seen. I know you already see me and know me through and through. Love me to life in your warm embrace as I come to you.

SHINE BRIGHT

"No one lights a lamp and hides it in a clay jar or puts it under a bed. Instead, they put it on a stand, so that those who come in can see the light."

LUKE 8:16 NIV

Never let anyone put out your light. When you feel you are too much, don't shrink yourself to fit others' expectations. When you feel you aren't enough, don't try to make up for it by conforming to others' ideals.

Jesus has set you free in his love. You are uniquely and wonderfully made! When you live in the light of his mercy, you are free to be you in all your you-ness. There is so much room in his love for you to shine. You were made to glow. Like the moon reflects the sun's brightness at night, so do we reflect his light in our lives. Let go of the need to please others and seek to please God just the way you were created to.

Jesus, thank you for your liberating love. I don't want to shrink or conform to the standards of anyone who is not you. I trust that your mercy is big enough for me. I don't need to be anyone or anything that I am not. I look to you, and I rise up to shine without shame.

BETTER HOPE

The hope of the righteous ends in gladness,
but the expectation of the wicked comes to nothing.

PROVERBS 10:28 NRSV

As we get curious about the motives of our hopes, we may find underlying belief systems in our hearts that we had no idea existed. We are all products of our environments, and we cannot escape the conditioning of our communities, families, and cultures. When it comes to our hope, may we align it in the light of who Jesus was, is, and always will be.

When you think of a wicked person, what traits come to mind? When you think of a righteous person, what values and traits do they possess? As you look into the Scriptures, and more specifically into Jesus' teachings, may you find revelation of righteousness and deeper understanding. May all your hopes find their source and fulfillment in him.

Jesus, I don't want to put my hopes in vain pursuits that don't have their beginning or end in you. Teach me in your truth and guide me with your wisdom. I will rely on you.

JOYFUL SALVATION

With joy you will drink deeply
from the fountain of salvation.

ISAIAH 12:3 NLT

Have you known the joy of God's help in your life? Have you tasted the goodness of his salvation? Through Christ, you have an open door to the Father. Yes, you have an invitation to the throne of God! He welcomes you with open arms, and he will not turn you away when you come to him.

In John 3:16, Jesus said that God showed how he loved the world when he sent his one and only Son. Whoever believes in him will have eternal life. This is the joy of our salvation: knowing that we have been offered everlasting, abundant, joyful, and fulfilling life in Christ who came to set us free in the love of the Father. What a glorious inheritance we will share with him in his coming kingdom. What a day to look forward to!

Jesus, thank you for everlasting life in you. I have given you leadership over my life and yielded my heart to you, and I believe you are the Son of God. May I experience joy in the fountain of your salvation today.

UNDER HIS SMILE

Smile on me, your servant.
Let your undying love and glorious grace
save me from all this gloom.

PSALM 31:16 TPT

Have you had a hard day, week, or season where you could not seem to escape heavy gloom? Certainly, pain is a part of life. Suffering is a given, but we should not put it on a pedestal or expect to only suffer in life. Jesus assured us that we would go through trials of many kinds, and he offers us peace in the midst of them. As the seasons pass, our circumstances shift and change.

May you experience the smile of God today lifting the weighty gloom of your present troubles. The weight of the world is not yours to carry. His undying love and glorious grace surround you, and they have the power to lift the heavy burdens you are carrying. May God shine his face on you, and may you be covered in the glory of his presence.

Jesus, you are my Savior and the lifter of my head. I trust you more than the bad reports that seem to be broadcast ceaselessly. I trust that you are still working in this world and in my life, and I ask you to radiate your love on me today.

KEEP LIVING IN LOVE

Though you have not seen him, you love him; and even though you do not see him now, you believe in him and are filled with an inexpressible and glorious joy.

1 PETER 1:8 NIV

There is so much value in choosing to live your life in the abiding and overwhelming love of Christ. "Though you have not seen him, you love him." May you continue to choose him over and over again. He is worthy of every sacrifice and surrender. His love is pure and his motives untainted. He does not push or override your choices. He does not manipulate or abuse.

He sees every move you make whether you have noted them or not. He sees the motivations of your heart and your choices. He knows what moves you. He knows what keeps you up at night. You can trust his love. He does not seek to control you; he sets you free in the liberty of his mercy. May you live into that freedom more and more and continue to choose love in all things.

Jesus, I love you. I choose to keep coming after you no matter how many times I fall. I know your love is better than any other. You set me truly free.

HE WILL DO IT

All of God's promises have been fulfilled in Christ
with a resounding "Yes!" And through Christ,
our "Amen" ascends to God for his glory.

2 CORINTHIANS 1:20 NLT

What God has promised, he will do. What he has
committed to, he will follow through on. May we find
our confidence in his nature, his faithfulness, and his
unrelenting love. May we press on to be more like him as
we get to know him more.

When you make a promise, what are the chances that
you will follow through on it? Loyal friends are few and
treasured. May you be a person of your word, and when
you fail, may you be humble in asking for understanding
and admitting your limits. Even when you fail, God will not.
He is so much greater than we humans are.

*Jesus, you are the yes and amen to all of God's promises.
You are the fulfillment of every longing. I trust you to
continue to fulfill your Word and follow through on each
vow you have made. May I be loyal in love just as you are.*

WONDERFUL WORKS

His unforgettable works of surpassing wonder
reveal his grace and tender mercy.

PSALM 111:4 TPT

When our hearts are weary, we can be encouraged by remembering what God has already done. May we look through history's lens with curiosity and retell the stories of God's faithfulness. God still moves in wonderful ways. What breakthroughs and victories, both big and small, have we quickly forgotten and moved on from?

As we remember the wonderful things God has done, may we be encouraged to praise him. He is full of grace and tender mercy. He has not stopped faithfully following through on his Word. He is just, he is full of truth, and he continues to move with the limitless lengths of his love.

Jesus, remind me of your power. Refresh me in your wonder-working presence. Thank you for the miraculous ways you have moved. I'm grateful for this foretaste and indicator of greater things to come.

WAIT IN HOPE

If we look forward to something we don't yet have,
we must wait patiently and confidently.

ROMANS 8:25 NLT

We cannot escape the waiting seasons of life. Whether it's the moments before a doctor's visit or the time it takes to develop a practice from a plan, patience and confidence will serve us well. Patience does not look like passive avoidance. It does not mean that we do nothing. It means that we learn to appreciate the journey from one thing to the next.

May our confidence always be directed toward Christ. He is the overcomer, and through him, we also overcome. As we wait, he is our strength. As we work at what we have while hoping for more, he is our constant source of help. With him, waiting turns to rejoicing and expectant hope.

Jesus, there is more hope in you than I could ever find outside of you. I long to know you more and be found in your loyal love in every season of the soul. Fill me with strength and confidence as I continue to lean on you for all I need.

SPOKEN INTO EXISTENCE

The LORD merely spoke, and the heavens were created.
He breathed the word, and all the stars were born.

PSALM 33:6 NLT

It takes no more than a creative thought and word for
God to speak into existence what wasn't merely a moment
before. His power exceeds our imaginations, and his
creativity knows no bounds. May we be encouraged in his
ability to create with merely a breath.

Every star in the sky started as a thought. Every person
on the planet was intentionally made in the imagination
of God. Rather than doubting the significance of our
lives, may we be encouraged that God did not make any
mistakes when he made us. We are fearfully, wonderfully,
and lovingly created. May we press into his presence even
more, letting his truth build up our identities and break
down the lies of shame.

*Jesus, in you, all my shame has been disarmed. You
lovingly welcome me to the Father's throne. I come to you
with my heart wide open and my mind ready to receive
greater revelations of your mercy.*

CAREFUL WORDS

Those who are careful about what they say
keep themselves out of trouble.

PROVERBS 21:23 NCV

How careful are you about the words you speak? Not just when you are talking to someone, but also when you talk about them? Jesus said in Luke 6:45, "People speak the things that are in their hearts." We should not simply be concerned with what we say but also why we say it.

Take this opportunity to be careful about what you say, and may you also evaluate the fruit of your thoughts and reactions. We know God does not simply look to what we do. He sees the core of our hearts: our motivations and intentions. In his mercy, we can be continually transformed into his love both with our actions and with our hearts.

Jesus, I don't want to miss the point of your wisdom. I don't want to paint a pretty picture to present to others and miss the deep work of heart-healing and alignment. Show me where my thoughts are not aligned in your mercy; I am open to you.

YOU ALREADY KNOW

He has told you what he wants from you:
to do what is right to other people,
love being kind to others,
and live humbly, obeying your God.

MICAH 6:8 NCV

The gospel of Christ is simple. It is attainable. It is accessible to all. God is not a demanding master who moves the mark constantly to keep us guessing at what he wants from us. *He has told you what he wants from you.* You already know.

May you use the verse for today as a guidepost to keep pressing into the things that matter and let go of all that doesn't. Simply *do what is right to other people, love being kind to others, and live humbly, obeying your God.* It really is that simple.

Jesus, thank you for the fellowship of your presence. Thank you for the reminder that your expectations of me are simple and your grace is sufficient for me. I will take your Word to heart today and live according to your wisdom.

UNBREAKABLE TRUST

Those who know your name trust in you,
for you, Lord, have never forsaken those who seek you.

Psalm 9:10 NIV

No matter what, keep trusting in the Lord. He won't give up on you, he won't abandon you, and he will never turn you away. Keep going after him and seeking after his heart. He is not hard to find. Wherever you find the fruit of his Spirit, he is there. Wherever you find true peace, rest, joy, love, and acceptance, he is in your midst.

You can truly trust him. Even when you are faithless, he is still faithful. His goodness is not dependent on your belief. Your heart can know rest in his unfailing love. Instead of insisting on carrying the weight of your worries, you can let go and trust him with the unknowns you can't control. He is with you, and he is for you.

Jesus, I trust you. I trust you with my hopes and my disappointments. I trust you with my greatest triumphs and my greatest defeats. I believe you will rebuild, repair, and redeem what I thought was wasted. I know nothing is wasted in your mercy.

RELYING ON FAITHFULNESS

I have always been mindful of your unfailing love
and have lived in reliance on your faithfulness.

PSALM 26:3 NIV

When we rely on the faithfulness of God, it is not foolishness but wisdom. Though we can make our plans and execute them to the best of our ability, we cannot control the future. We cannot ensure a favorable outcome. There will always be variables at play in the world and in this life that we do not know to consider.

But God is faithful. He sees it all; he knows it, and he knows you. He is never surprised, and he isn't thrown off-course. He will continue to move in merciful kindness and in the power of his love. What he has set in motion, no one can deter. Trust him. He is faithful.

Jesus, I will live today with reliance on your faithfulness, confidence in your unfailing love, and trust in your sovereignty. I let go of the need to anxiously ruminate on what I can't control, and I let you take the lead.

THE ONLY WAY

"I am the way, the truth, and the life.
No one can come to the Father except through me."

JOHN 14:6 NLT

Why should we exhaust ourselves by trying to find our way to purity, goodness, and unending mercy when we already have the path of life in front of us? Jesus has invited us into fellowship with the Father through himself. Through union with Jesus Christ, we have an open door to the Father's presence.

Even now, the Spirit leads us in faith. May we look to Jesus who is both the originator and the finisher of our faith. There is nothing more we need to do. We don't have to ready ourselves, put on our best outfits, or clean up the mess of our lives. We simply come. We follow Jesus: the way, the truth, and the life.

Jesus, you are the way to the Father. I believe it. I turn toward you and away from the lure of selfish ambition. I want to know you more. I want to know the pure delight of the Father's heart. I want to know your longing for justice, mercy, and truth to prevail. I want you.

OVERFLOWING WITH MERCY

"Show mercy and compassion for others,
just as your heavenly Father overflows
with mercy and compassion for all."

LUKE 6:36 TPT

There is no end to the mercy and compassion the Father continually pours out on us. Why, then, are we so quick to cut off our own? Why should we slam doors and erect walls in the name of Christ? It goes against his very nature to do so.

When we open our hearts in compassion and extend mercy to others, whether or not we perceive them as "deserving" of such kindness, we reflect the love that God extends to us. God is kind to all, not just to the friendly and open. To all. Jesus loved his enemies as fully as he loved his closest friends. May we be found like him and do the same.

Jesus, I know there is no excuse for my lack of love toward some people. I don't want to harbor grudges or double down on my disdain. Soften my heart in your love. Empower me to offer mercy and kindness to those I struggle to like.

LEARN FROM HIM

"Take my yoke upon you and learn from me,
for I am gentle and humble in heart,
and you will find rest for your souls."

MATTHEW 11:29 NIV

What kind of leader are you drawn to? Is it someone who is charismatic and loud? Someone who tends to lead by example? There are many leadership styles, and the style itself is not an indicator of a person's heart, their motivations, or the substance of what they are offering.

Jesus is true. He is full of unfailing wisdom, and he is not forceful. He is gentle, trustworthy, and humble, yet he has all the answers. He does not need to shout to be heard. He does not need to demean someone to uplift himself or anyone else. No matter what personality traits we admire in others, may we value the substance of a person's life, the fruit of their work, and their personal integrity above all else.

Jesus, I'm so glad you are not domineering. I love that you give space to your followers and friends for us to make our own choices. You are not threatened by freedom; you offer true liberation. I follow you, and I want my soul to know its true rest in your love.

TODAY'S BLESSING

May he give you the desire of your heart
and make all your plans succeed.

PSALM 20:4 NIV

Whatever you are longing for, may you find it. May God give you the desire of your heart. May he bless the work of your hands. May he make all your plans succeed as you continually surrender to his leadership.

Above all, may you know the all-surpassing goodness of knowing Christ. He is the source of every good gift, and his faithfulness is uninterrupted by the troubles of this world. Though your life may change and shift with the seasons and the times, his love never does. He is unfailing in mercy. He will continue to move in powerful ways.

Jesus, I trust you with my deepest desires. I have given you leadership of my life, and I trust you to bless the work of my hands and bring it all together in your merciful redemption. Have your way in my life, Lord. Be glorified.

HIGHER THAN THE HEAVENS

As high as the heavens are above the earth,
so great is his steadfast love toward those who fear him.

PSALM 103:11 ESV

When the worries of this world pile up, may we take the lead of the psalmist and look up to the heavens. As far as they reach, God's love reaches further. In the abundant expanse of the universe, God's mercy fills every space. It is constantly expanding, multiplying in its power, even as our universe is expanding.

Our grief and our problems are real too. The loyal and steadfast love of God is also real. It extends much further than the reaches of our imaginations. It goes further than our projected fears. May we step outside our small lives and into the possibility of greater realities. The great kingdom of Christ is our ultimate home, and we can rest our hearts in him even as we wait for him to return.

Jesus, I want to see from your higher perspective today. Whenever I get overwhelmed by the problems in and around me, I will step outside and breathe in the space that meets me. I will remember that I am but a small part of a larger whole and that your love is limitless.

RIGHTEOUS LIVING

"Seek the Kingdom of God above all else, and live righteously, and he will give you everything you need."

MATTHEW 6:33 NLT

Jesus' instruction to "seek the Kingdom of God above all else" follows the admonition to not worry about what we eat or drink or wear. Instead of channeling our energy into worrying about possible outcomes that are out of our control, let's trust God to provide for us as the good Father he already is and seek him.

When we seek the kingdom of God first, we look to his values above this world's. When we make righteous living our goal, everything we need falls into place. Let's live with integrity, honor, and mercy. Let's choose kindness instead of selfish ambition. Righteousness is found in Christ, and we do not rely on our own merit to gain it. Let's align our lives in Christ and trust God to provide for what we need. He will do it.

Jesus, I am looking to live for your kingdom first and foremost. Your kingdom is above every system in this world including every religious structure. I choose you, and I press into your presence now. Transform me in your lovingkindness as I look to you.

CONSISTENT EFFORT

"Everyone who asks will receive.
The one who searches will find.
And everyone who knocks will have the door opened."

LUKE 11:10 NCV

No matter how comfortable or desperate you feel today, may you look to the Lord. He meets you with the abundance of his marvelous mercy no matter what state you are in. He is with you even now. Ask him for what you need. Search him out and you will find him. He is closer than you realize. Knock on heaven's door, and he will open it for you.

There is beauty in the simplicity of fellowship with Jesus. We do not have to pray perfectly, do things just right, or pretend to be what we are not. Jesus covers us with his overwhelmingly perfect love and accepts us as we are. Do not give up today. Keep moving even if it's at a snail's pace. Your consistent effort will always be met by the abundance of God's mercy in Christ.

Jesus, thank you for being consistent in your pursuit of my heart. I will not turn away or get distracted by things that don't matter. I want to know you more. Speak to me, answer me, and meet with me now.

GOOD SHEPHERD

"I am the good shepherd.
The good shepherd lays his life down for the sheep."

JOHN 10:11 ESV

Jesus is the Good Shepherd. What does that mean for us? A shepherd is a caretaker, but he is also a warrior. Shepherds fight off those who seek to kill and destroy the flock. Lions, bears, any predator that would prey on the sheep: they cannot scare a good shepherd away. In fact, he is willing to lay down his life for his sheep.

Jesus was willing to do this for us. He did it. He laid down his very life so that we could be spared. He wrestled death and lost, but he was not dead for long. Death was conquered, and it lost its power when Jesus rose three days later. He is now living, and his life is ours. He not only saved us, but he set us free from death's stronghold in the process. Now, we have eternal life to look forward to in his glorious kingdom.

Jesus, thank you for facing my fears and for saving me from the curse of sin and death. You have overcome every enemy I face, and I partner with you to stand in your victory. I trust you to continue to guide me through this life and keep me safe.

LET IT GO

"Forget the former things;
do not dwell on the past."

ISAIAH 43:18 NIV

Guilt can trap us in a cycle of overthinking. We all have our moments where shame takes the wheel of our minds and steers us to familiar places we would rather not go. Just because something is familiar does not make it right.

May we take to heart the words of God through the prophet Isaiah as we let go of what we cannot change. *Forget the former things; do not dwell on the past.* He's doing a new thing. We can't change a thing through introspection of things that are in our history. Shame grabs hold of us and equates our mistakes with our worth, but Christ has liberated us from shame. He has the final say on who we are. We are worthy of love in this moment, and he has not changed his mind about us. He never will.

Jesus, when I start to get caught up in shame-based thinking, will you help me to reframe my thoughts in your truth? You say I am worthy of love. You created me, and you did it with purpose. You don't hold my mistakes against me, so I will let go of what I cannot change and trust you with my present and future.

PERSISTENCE IS KEY

Patient endurance is what you need now,
so that you will continue to do God's will.
Then you will receive all that he has promised.

HEBREWS 10:36 NLT

When you have run out of motivation, there is a key you can hold on to for consistency. When you are no longer excited about what you are doing but the task is still necessary, patient endurance is vital. Persistence is key to your success no matter what that success is.

Motivation is helpful to get you started, but it will not be what keeps you going. What keeps you going is focus and vision, but also the willingness to just keep at it. The in-between times are not lauded or celebrated, but they are necessary. Jesus' ministry was not all mountaintop experiences. Surely, he did not feel like getting up every morning, but he did it to spend time with the Father. Whatever it is you are struggling to follow through on today, may you be encouraged to keep moving through. With or without motivation, you can persist.

Jesus, thank you for the practical reminder of persistence in your kingdom. I will not give up spending time with you, and I won't lose sight of the things I need to keep pushing through in life. I trust you to continue to be my help and vision.

I BELIEVE

I remain confident of this:
I will see the goodness of the LORD
in the land of the living.

PSALM 27:13 NIV

The Lord has not stopped being good just because we struggle to recognize his goodness in our circumstances. He has not stopped working his mercy in our lives even if we cannot spot it as easily as we once did. He is forever faithful, always overflowing in loyal love, and never weary.

Though our moods and energy constantly shift, Jesus is steady and constant. He is not easily upset, and he does not threaten to remove his presence from us when we waver. No matter how little or how much faith we have at the moment, let's remember that God is faithful. May our confidence rest in his constant character. On our good days and our bad days, may we recite with the psalmist, "I remain confident of this: I will see the goodness of the LORD in the land of the living."

Jesus, you are my confidence and my strength. You are my hope and where all my satisfaction lies. I trust you to continue to work out your goodness in my life and in this world. I know you are not finished yet!

PERFECTED IN CHRIST

By that one offering he forever made perfect
those who are being made holy.

HEBREWS 10:14 NLT

Before Christ's sacrifice, animal sacrifices were required to atone for sins in the old covenant that Israel had with the Lord. Christ's sacrifice replaced the old covenant with a completely new one. In this covenant, no more sacrifices are required. We have, once and for all, been made holy by the blood of Jesus.

Whatever faults you find in yourself, whatever flaws you struggle to accept, know this: in Christ, you have already been made perfect in his mercy. With your life yielded to his leadership, you need never question whether you need to do more, be more, or perform more. You are perfected, and you are complete in him. Let his love continually transform you, for you are free from the curse of sin and alive in Christ.

Jesus, you are my liberator and my loving leader. I submit my life to yours, for I know you are good. Thank you for taking responsibility of our holiness and for welcoming us into your family with mercy and grace. I am yours.

CONTINUAL SURRENDER

Continue to walk surrendered to the extravagant love of Christ, for he surrendered his life as a sacrifice for us. His great love for us was pleasing to God, like an aroma of adoration—a sweet healing fragrance.

EPHESIANS 5:2 TPT

Surrender is often seen as weakness in this world. Humility and a compassionate heart are often ridiculed by the powerful. However, there is nothing more powerful than a surrendered life lived with love. Jesus lived surrendered to the Father. He chose mercy when those around him would choose judgment or apathy.

May we, too, live with hearts surrendered to the love of God. He is our source and our strength. We live out of the overflow of his love toward us, and we can freely offer others the same compassion we have received. May we continually submit our hearts to Christ, for he is worthy of our adoration and trust.

Jesus, thank you for the example of your love. I can look to it when I am overwhelmed by the weight and responsibilities of this world. Your love is my guide instead of the rhetoric of those who hold power. I choose to surrender to you in loving trust. Continue to guide me into your goodness.

PAY ATTENTION

Be not quick in your spirit to become angry,
for anger lodges in the heart of fools.

ECCLESIASTES 7:9 ESV

Anger is a good indicator that something is off. Anger is not a sin. It's what we do with it, how we react to others, that can lead to harm and sin. Instead of dismissing it or wishing it away, let's get curious around the areas of our hearts and lives where we are dealing with anger.

Pay attention to what angers you. Is there a common thread or theme? What kinds of actions send you overboard? Anger can arise out of many situations. Perhaps you need better boundaries around your time and energy. Perhaps you need to be aware of when you are hungry or tired. When we allow ourselves to react in anger or harbor it in our hearts against others, it will lead to harm. Once we realize it is an indicator of areas where we feel unseen, out of control, or where injustice is rampant, we can approach it and ourselves differently.

Jesus, I don't want to be quick to anger or hold a grudge. Show me what is at the root of the anger that crops up in my life. Give me wisdom to adjust my boundaries when necessary. Shoe me when to simply let go of offense. Thank you.

GARDENS OF JOY

Those who sow with tears
will reap with songs of joy.

PSALM 126:5 NIV

No tear that you have ever cried is forgotten. No anguish
you have felt is overlooked by the Lord. Though you
cannot escape the painful experiences that come with
humanity and living in the world we do, there is hope even
in your sorrow.

Jesus is our Redeemer. He takes what breaks us down and
builds us up with new life. When we feel broken beyond
repair, his love expands to fill every crack and crevice and
sow new life with hope and promise. He is so much better
than we can imagine. He is not finished sowing his mercy
into the soil of our lives even when the soil is full of ashes
of defeat and disappointment. There is new life on its way.
It will bloom, and we will reap that garden of glory with
songs of joy.

*Jesus, thank you for always working even when I cannot
perceive it. I trust you to continue to redeem what seems
irredeemable. Restore what feels utterly lost. You are
better than I can imagine, and I put my hope in you.*

SEPTEMBER

The Lord within it is righteous;
he does no wrong.
Every morning he renders his judgment,
each dawn without fail;
but the unjust knows no shame.

ZEPHANIAH 3:5 NRSV

THANKFUL HEART

Devote yourselves to prayer
with an alert mind and a thankful heart.

COLOSSIANS 4:2 NLT

Prayer does not require the perfect sentiments or a specific style. It is an open door of communication between us and heaven. Prayer is bigger than a statement we make in cathedrals. It is more than a request we make in desperation. It can be as constant as our breathing. Our lives can be an open conversation with the Creator.

Devotion is nothing more than giving our loving attention to something. When we devote ourselves to prayer, may we do it with intention and thanksgiving. It is less about what we say or offer and more about the one we are praying to. We know Jesus is full of mercy, and we can expect to be met by his love every time we turn to him in prayer.

Jesus, I give you my loving attention. I invite you to continue to speak to me, lead me in life, and get my attention when I am distracted. Thank you for the beauty of fellowship with you through your Spirit. I long to know you more.

ARMED WITH STRENGTH

It is God who arms me with strength
and keeps my way secure.

PSALM 18:32 NIV

If we feel alone in our endeavors, let us remember that God walks with us, strengthens us, and leads us. We are never really alone. The Spirit of God is our companion. The Spirit offers us comfort when we're grieving, perspective when our own is clouded, joy in the presence of the Lord, and wisdom whenever we ask for it.

When we go through unchartered territory, he clears the path ahead of us. When night falls and it is hard to see, he is the light who leads us step by step. He is trustworthy, he is powerful, and he is faithful. Let us take courage in his company and refuge in his living peace.

Jesus, you are the one who arms me with strength when I am weak. You keep me secure as I follow you. Even when my world is turned upside-down, you never change. I trust you.

BE OPEN TO CORRECTION

Listen to advice and accept correction,
and in the end you will be wise.

PROVERBS 19:20 NCV

It is important that we not become too wise in our own eyes. We need room to grow, learn, and transform into people of love, justice, and mercy. If we want to walk in the ways of Jesus under his leadership, then we are subject to his correction.

Jesus corrected his followers and friends, and we should expect the same. His correction does not leave us degraded in shame; it encourages us to grow in our faith. Jesus rebuked his disciples for their lack of faith when they were weathering the storm on the boat. He even corrected Peter's jealousy of John by encouraging him to focus on himself. If Jesus corrected his disciples, he will also correct us. Let's remember he does it because he loves us.

Jesus, I don't want to be too proud to receive correction. When you challenge me, even that is done with kindness. I'm so grateful for your better way. I humble myself before you as I continue to follow your loving lead.

DELIGHTED IN

The LORD takes delight in his people;
he crowns the humble with victory.

PSALM 149:4 NIV

As children of the living God, we are not only given a place in his kingdom; we are also delighted in by our good Father. Have you ever witnessed the delight of parents over their children? God is full of passionate love for us, and his joy over us does not diminish.

Your Father delights in what you offer him. Just as a parent delights in the humble offerings that a child gives them, whether it be a drawing or an afternoon snack, your Father delights in you the same way. He knows you better than you know anyone, and he really, really likes who you are. May you be encouraged in the heart of your Father today as he reveals his heart to you in greater measure.

Jesus, will you show me in real, tangible ways how the Father delights in me? I want to be loved to life in your presence today. I love you.

TRANSFORMED MIND

Do not be shaped by this world; instead be changed
within by a new way of thinking. Then you will be able
to decide what God wants for you; you will know what
is good and pleasing to him and what is perfect.

ROMANS 12:2 NCV

Have you evaluated the fruit of your thoughts lately? Have
you taken time to observe what your mind is consumed
with? Get curious around your thoughts today. Are you
filled with anxiety? If so, consider how much news you
have been consuming. Are you feeling inadequate? Look at
how much time you have spent scrolling on social media.

In today's age where information and non-stop
entertainment is at our fingertips, it is important to take
breaks from technology to focus and fill our minds with
what actually matters to us. Our minds will make meaning
out of what we fill it with, so let's fill it with intention. May
Christ be our greatest influence and teacher.

*Jesus, I know what I put in my mind matters. I don't want
to be shaped by the world but by you and your kingdom
truth. I focus my heart and mind on you, and I ask for
your help to set up boundaries around the information I
consume. Please, bring balance to my life.*

A WILLING SPIRIT

Let my passion for life be restored,
tasting joy in every breakthrough you bring to me.
Hold me close to you with a willing spirit
that obeys whatever you say.

PSALM 51:12 TPT

When we are having a rough go of things, the psalms are a great place for encouragement. David and the other psalmists did not shrink back from displaying the whole of the human experience. It is not a sin to struggle emotionally; it is human.

When you find yourself struggling, spend some time in Psalms. There, you will find something that feels familiar to what you are going through. Perhaps hearing how the poets turn their suffering into praise will help you do the same.

Jesus, I'm so grateful to know I am not alone in my struggle. You wept, you were tired and hungry, and you knew heartbreak and pure joy. I trust that in my experiences, I will find how you relate. I love you, Lord, and I will keep on following you.

NONE TOO SMALL

"I tell you the truth, anything you did for even the least of my people here, you also did for me."

MATTHEW 25:40 NCV

The Lord looks over creation and does not miss anything. He does not overlook anyone. We should never be so proud as to think any human being is expendable to him. He loves with fierce devotion, and he will not let the vulnerable waste away.

Let's be more like Jesus and reach beyond our spheres. Let's advocate for the vulnerable, feed the hungry, and clothe the poor. Let's not spend so much time in our safe spaces that we mistake different for unworthy. Following the laid-down love of Jesus will not keep us comfortable. May we help those who need it without the need for recognition or recompense. May we do it for love and not to be heroes. May we be the hands and feet of Jesus. What we do for others, we do for him.

Jesus, correct my misperceptions in the truth of your mercy. I don't want to idolize my comfort above another's humanity and rights. I choose to follow you on your path of love no matter where it takes me. You are worthy of every surrender.

IN THE MORNING

"Now is your time of grief, but I will see you again and you will rejoice, and no one will take away your joy."

JOHN 16:22 NIV

We cannot escape the seasons of grief that deep loss brings. Through every trial and transition, the Spirit is near to comfort and uphold us. Jesus is our healer, and he won't stop tending to our wounds even as they continue to appear from the battles we face in life.

If now is your time of grief, remember that joy comes in the morning. It will come. Sorrow won't defeat or diminish you. It will not be this intense forever. Though it may be hard to believe, his mercy sows seeds that will grow new life in this space. You may not be able to see it clearly until you are on the other side, but you will see. You will rejoice. You will know him more and have more compassion and empathy. Hold on in the middle of your dark night. Morning will come.

Jesus, thank you for your comfort. I look to you in every season of the soul. In my grief, be my comfort. In my peace, may I be a comfort to others. I trust joy will come again.

HE HAS DONE IT

He was wounded for our transgressions, crushed for our iniquities; upon him was the punishment that made us whole, and by his bruises we are healed.

ISAIAH 53:5 NRSV

Everything Jesus endured, from his arrest to the torment he faced on the cross, was utterly brutal. It was also just hours away from his, and our, redemption. When we walk through fiery trials of all kinds, we have the promise of redemption. Whatever end may be looming in front of us, it is not our actual end.

Jesus overcame death, and he is our salvation and our hope. He is our Redeemer. He conquered the shadows of sin and death that laid claim on our souls; he set us free from the darkness of despair. We have been made alive in his love, and we live in the incarnate power of his resurrection. Whatever we face, we are more than conquerors through Christ.

Jesus, thank you for your sacrifice. I cannot begin to understand the depths of it, yet I am humbled and compelled to thank you. You are my hope and my healing. You are my Redeemer.

ALL I NEED

The LORD is my shepherd;
I have everything I need.

PSALM 23:1 NCV

With the Lord Jesus as our shepherd, we have everything
we need. He takes care of us, watches over us, directs us,
and fights our enemies. When we wander astray, he comes
to find us. When we are unable to move, he carries us. He
is kind, attentive, and strong. He will lead us to refreshing
waters, and he will take care of all our earthly needs.

Do you trust Jesus as your Good Shepherd? Do you truly
believe he will provide for your needs? Or do you waste
away with worry over what tomorrow will bring? Let today
be today and fix your eyes on Jesus. He is the giver of life,
and he loves you fiercely. He will not let you fall outside of
his reach. You can trust him. You can take rest in his care.
He has perfect peace to spare, and he will keep you in his
perfect love.

*Jesus, I want to trust you more than I worry. I want to be
confident in your character more than I wonder about what
will happen in the future. Guide me with your peace and
calm me with your near presence. Help me to stay grateful
in this moment and in this day that you have made.*

UNASHAMED

Hope does not put us to shame, because God's love has been poured into our hearts through the Holy Spirit who has been given to us.

ROMANS 5:5 ESV

It is not foolish to put our hope in Christ. He is greater than our circumstances. He is outside of time and space and not limited by the confines of our world. He is full of mercy that sets captives free, heals the sick, and raises the dead.

Let us courageously continue to put our hope in him. He is loyal to his Word, and he is faithful to every promise he has made. When we waver, he stands firm. When we are full of doubt, he is still constant in truth. The Holy Spirit is our help in all things, and that includes believing. Let's lean into the presence of our God and put all our hope in Jesus.

Jesus, I believe you are the way, the truth, and the life. I believe you will do everything you have set out to do even if it looks different than we expect. I put all my hope in you, for you are full of pure love and marvelous mercy.

HELD

"Don't be afraid, for I am with you.
Don't be discouraged, for I am your God.
I will strengthen you and help you.
I will hold you up with my victorious right hand."

ISAIAH 41:10 NLT

Why do you think that God instructs his people to not be afraid more than 300 times in his Word? Isn't it because we are prone, in our humanity, to be overrun by fear? We should not be ashamed when fear rises up, but we also do not have to be victims.

Christ has overcome every fear by his victory on the cross. His resurrection power loosened the grip of fear over our lives. In Christ, we are free to live with his unshakeable triumph. We have been brought to life in his life, and he has promised to always be with us. When we are afraid, let's take courage in his presence with us. He will strengthen us and help us; he will continue to hold us close.

Jesus, thank you for the reminder of your nearness. You are my courage and my strength. Hold me close in your love and cover me with your perfect peace. I rely on you, and I will not let fear's voice drown out your whispers.

THEY'RE JUST PEOPLE

We can say with confidence, "The Lord is my helper,
so I will have no fear. What can mere people do to me?"

HEBREWS 13:6 NLT

It is a bold statement to say, "What can mere people do
to me?" It reflects a confidence in the Lord's help that
transcends our mortal bodies and experiences. People
can do a lot to harm us! This verse does not dismiss that
possibility. It is recognition of a place in us that no person
can control. Our souls are our own, and we get to choose
whom we will trust.

When you are tempted to fear others, may you be
grounded in the truth that they are only people. They may
have more power than you, but they are not more special.
They may be able to come against you, but they cannot
come against God in you. May you cling to the Lord and his
help in all things. Don't let fear lead you; let your soul rely
on the Lord.

*Jesus, I trust you more than I trust any other. You are
faithful, and I will not let fear convince me otherwise. Be
my strength, my courage, and my wise leader in all things.
I will continue to trust you.*

LEAVE SOME SPACE

Always be humble and gentle. Be patient with each other, making allowance for each other's faults because of your love.

EPHESIANS 4:2 NCV

No one is perfect: not you, not me, and not any person. Christ doesn't expect perfection from us, so why do we put that expectation on ourselves or others? The necessity for mercy, humility, and forgiveness comes from the fact that we all make mistakes. We will continue to make mistakes. How we repair relationships and own up to our flaws will reflect how humble we truly are as well as how willing we are to be like Christ.

Let's take this verse to heart. Let's seek to be humble and gentle with ourselves as well as with others. Compassion is a beautiful trait to carry in our hearts. Instead of letting perfectionism dictate how we tolerate mistakes, let's give patience room to grow. Let's allow space for each other's flaws instead of holding them against each other. There is strength in clear-minded kindness.

Jesus, thank you for your love that does not require perfection. I don't want to hold myself or others to an unrealistic expectation. As I let go of it, I make room for your love to blossom and grow in my relationships. Help me let go of perfection today.

HE SEES

You keep track of all my sorrows.
You have collected all my tears in your bottle.
You have recorded each one in your book.

PSALM 56:8 NLT

God does not track only our victories and successes; he also records every one of our sorrows. His love is not greater in our joy than it is in our grief. His love is always overflowing and always reaching toward us. He sees our tears, and he understands them.

Isaiah 53:3 says Jesus was a man of sorrows, acquainted with deepest grief. Jesus keeps record of our personal troubles, and he experienced deepest grief and incredible sorrow himself. He understands our losses. He understands our sadness. May we never forget that he is God who lived the extent of the human experience. He gets it. There is solace in his companionship.

Jesus, I'm relieved to know you do not overlook or ignore my sorrow. You do not turn away from my hard emotions. You are with me in it all, and you understand what it is like. Thank you, Lord.

LIGHT OF LIFE

"I am the light of the world. Whoever follows me will not walk in darkness, but will have the light of life."

JOHN 8:12 ESV

When we choose to follow Jesus, we walk in the glowing steps of the Creator of this world. He will not lead us into darkness, and the darkness of this world will not push us. He is the light of the world. He is the sun, radiating warmth and light and giving life to everything he touches. When we look to him, he lights the way. Everything becomes clearer in his presence.

May we embrace Jesus as the light of our lives. May we turn to him as sunflowers turn to the sun. He is our lifegiving source of strength and growth. He is the one who brings clarity with his perfect wisdom. In him, there is no shadow. He is all we need, everything we're searching for, and so much more. Let's not stop turning to him.

Jesus, thank you for your lifegiving light. You are my hope, my strength, and my source. You are my song, and I worship you with my choices. I love you more than I can express.

HE'S GOT YOU

He will not let you stumble;
the one who watches over you will not slumber.

PSALM 121:3 NLT

When we are worried, it can keep us from resting in God's peace. Our minds try to make sense of what possibilities lie in our futures and what we can do about them, but in reality, we cannot know what will happen. We can make plans, but only God knows how they will work out. After we have done what we are able to do, let's learn to rest in God's ability to take care of us.

He is a good father, and he never grows weary or distracted. He watches over us like a loving parent watches over a little one. We can trust that he won't miss a thing, and he can do far more and do it better than we could on our own. We can rest assured knowing that as we sleep, he is guarding us, and he continues to move in mercy.

Jesus, thank you for the reminder that you never grow tired. I lay down my worries, anxiety, and cares all before you, and I let go of the need to keep running through them. I rest in your peace because you hold me fast.

PRACTICE PATIENCE

Let patience have its perfect work, that you may be perfect and complete, lacking nothing.

JAMES 1:4 NKJV

The verse directly preceding the one we're focusing on today says that the testing of our faith produces the power of endurance within us. We don't need to be patient when everything is going our way. We don't need to endure the happy times; they are a joy to live.

Patience is necessary for the in-between moments between faith and fulfillment. It is built for the times of waiting when the testing of our faith happens. When we go through trials, we strengthen our souls by practicing endurance. God's favor is not found in the lack of problems in our lives but in his consistent presence with us through it all.

Jesus, sometimes patience doesn't come easily to me. I want to learn how to endure with grace and how to grab hold of the present and its gifts without wishing this time away. I trust you. Please, help me.

PEACEFUL HARVESTS

No discipline is enjoyable while it is happening—it's painful! But afterward there will be a peaceful harvest of right living for those who are trained in this way.

HEBREWS 12:11 NLT

When you hear the word "discipline," what does it evoke in you? What images or emotions come up? Before you equate your experience of what discipline has looked in your life with God's discipline, get curious about what the word means to you. If you were abused by a parent or a partner, your idea of discipline may be heavily skewed.

God's discipline looks like correction, and even his correction is laced with love. He never demeans or degrades you. He will not humiliate or hurt you. Correction is not fun to undergo, but it is necessary for life. It is painful because it is not what we want, but it should never look like abuse. Training stretches us past our comfort zones, but it does not seek to control us. God's ways are bigger and better than that.

Jesus, you are my peace. I want to live rightly and follow you in all I do. When I go astray, be my course correction. I invite your discipline in my life because I trust your character.

VICTORY SONGS

You are my hiding place;
you protect me from trouble.
You surround me with songs of victory.

PSALM 32:7 NLT

When we live our lives under the leadership of Christ, we allow him to teach, guide, and correct us. He is our hiding place, and he is also our truth. In the light of his life, we see more clearly the areas that do not align with his love. There is no excuse for us to follow Jesus and claim we are without sin. We all fall short, but his mercy covers us.

With humility, let's live before his gaze. Our victory comes from hiding ourselves in Christ. We do not earn our places in his kingdom. They are given to all out of the mercy of his heart. His grace is our sufficient strength, and his fellowship is our greatest gift. Let's stay in the safety of his presence no matter where our feet take us.

Jesus, you are my victory song. You are the one who makes me whole and who leads me into abundant life. You protect me from trouble, and you lead me into the goodness of your kingdom. Thank you.

PLANT GOOD SEEDS

Don't allow yourselves to be weary or disheartened in planting good seeds, for the season of reaping the wonderful harvest you've planted is coming!

GALATIANS 6:9 TPT

If we do not grow weary in doing good, our labor will pay off. After planting seeds of God's kingdom through loving acts of justice, truth, and compassion, we will reap the harvest of lives that are built on the foundation of Christ.

When it seems as if others are advancing in their lives without a care, let's remember that everyone has a different journey and timeline. Let's stay focused on our own gardens and plant seeds where we are and where God is leading us. Let's tend to the growth of our own lives and not be distracted by how others are choosing to live. God is with us in every step and season. He will not pass us by.

Jesus, I don't want to be so consumed with comparison that I forget and overlook the blessings I have right here and now. When it feels as if I am going backwards while others are pushing ahead, I will trust you and keep doing what is mine to do. You are my vision. Encourage my heart in your love today.

MUCH MORE

With God's power working in us, God can do much,
much more than anything we can ask or imagine.

EPHESIANS 3:21 NCV

By his lavish and endless love, God's mighty power is
working within us. It transcends our understanding and
overflows from us with the fullness of God. This power
transforms us in mercy, compassion, and understanding. It
gives us strength in our weakness, clarity in our confusion,
and hope in our disappointment.

God is able to do much, much more than we could even
dream of asking him to do. It is infinitely better than our
wildest imaginings. May we be encouraged to ask bigger,
live bolder, and be freer in this extravagant love of God
moving within our lives. His power is miraculous, and it
energizes us from the inside out.

Jesus, I praise you for your wonder-working power.
Continue to move in bigger and better ways than I can
imagine. I love you, I am yours, and I am expectant
that your love will continue to meet me, move me, and
transform me into your image.

VALIDATED

I will be glad and rejoice in your love,
for you saw my affliction
and knew the anguish of my soul.

PSALM 31:7 NIV

Have you ever kept a secret out of fear that no one would understand you? Have you refrained from sharing something because you had experienced others' disbelief or doubt in your experiences before? Even though others may not understand, Jesus does. He sees every affliction of your soul, both what is plain to the eye and what is hidden from others. He sees, knows, and understands you.

May you be covered in the love of God through Christ today. May you know the overwhelming acceptance of his wrap-around love that covers all your disappointment, regret, and shame. He will never deny you or your experience, but he also won't let you stay in it. He will heal, restore, and comfort you. He will transform and challenge you. In all this, he will love you to life, dear one.

Jesus, I cannot begin to thank you for the ways you see me. I am validated in your presence, and I come alive in your love. Heal me, Lord. Give me courage to be vulnerable with trusted friends in my life so that what has held me captive in the shadows may be disarmed in the light.

INCOMPARABLE WISDOM

Oh, how great are God's riches and wisdom and knowledge! How impossible it is for us to understand his decisions and his ways!

ROMANS 11:33 NLT

God's riches are much more than gold, jewels, and varied assets. His wealth is found in the incomparable wisdom and knowledge of his kingdom. Everything he does comes from a place of loyal love. He is constantly working in mercy. His justice is final, and he will set every wrong right in his perfect time.

Even when we cannot understand what he is doing, let's look to his constant character. Let's look for the fingerprints of his mercy in this world. Let's search for the clues of his kingdom that is founded on justice, truth, and righteousness. What he does is far better than any leader in this world. He is not power-hungry or vain. He sets us free to live in the light of his love, and so does his wisdom.

Jesus, I trust your wisdom more than I trust the wisdom of this world. I know my understanding is but in part, and I know you are working around the world in various ways. I will look for the fruit of your Spirit, and when I find it, I will know your wisdom is present.

PERFECT GIFTS

Whatever is good and perfect is a gift coming down to us from God our Father, who created all the lights in the heavens. He never changes or casts a shifting shadow.

JAMES 1:17 NLT

God is holy and pure. He never changes or casts a shifting shadow. He is constant, true, and righteous. He has nothing to hide! What God says, he means. This does not mean we always understand him fully though. God cannot be put in a box or system that we create to control or understand him. He is outside, above, and altogether too majestic for such a thing.

Let's accept the good gifts of this life as gifts from the Father. He gave us Jesus, the ultimate gift, through whom we come to him without fault. We don't need to try to decipher hidden codes from the wisdom of God. Though we try to complicate it, he speaks simply. May we wholeheartedly follow Christ, the purity of God and living expression of the Father. There is more goodness in him than we can find outside of him.

Jesus, you are the best gift I have ever received. Your friendship, help, and constant presence with me through your Spirit is what I need. Thank you for the blessings I have in my life. I'm grateful for all you do in loyal love.

SPIRITUAL RICHES TO SHARE

Our hearts ache, but we always have joy. We are poor, but we give spiritual riches to others. We own nothing, and yet we have everything.

2 CORINTHIANS 6:10 NLT

Even in heartache, we can experience the deep, abiding joy of knowing Christ. Even if we are poor, we have spiritual riches in Christ to offer others. Even if we do not own a thing, we have everything we long for in Christ.

Does this feel true to your experience? If so, how have you seen this play out in your life? If it feels foreign but is something that you want to know, consider readjusting your focus on what success looks like. Do you need to have a certain status in this world to feel fulfilled? Are you constantly looking to what you want to acquire in order to feel as if you have something to offer? If your focus is more on what is coming rather than what is, try practicing presence and gratitude throughout your day. Christ in you is the hope of glory.

Jesus, help me to remain rooted and grounded in your love today. I don't want to get ahead of myself or put my worth in something that is not mine at the moment. You are with me, and you are abundantly good. That is more than enough.

LEAVE IT THERE

Pour out all your worries and stress upon him and leave
them there, for he always tenderly cares for you.

1 PETER 5:7 TPT

Today is another day, another opportunity, to pour out
your worries and stress to God. Not only can you pour
them out on him, but you can leave them there. Don't carry
them with you once you have set them down. Christ cares
for you! He is full of tenderness toward you. Pour out all the
things that are weighing you down and let them go.

When Jesus said, "Are you weary, carrying a heavy burden?
Come to me. I will refresh your life. Simply join your life with
mine" in Matthew 11, he was inviting us to do what Peter
echoes in today's verse. We can lay down our burdens and
leave them there as we join our lives with Christ. There, we
will find refreshment and rest for our souls.

*Jesus, I lay down my heavy burdens, all my worries and
stress. at your feet. I give you my life and join it to yours.
Lead me, refresh me, and restore me in your peace-giving
love.*

ALL-SUFFICIENT ONE

I trust in the all-sufficient
cross of Christ alone.

1 CORINTHIANS 1:17 TPT

The message of the cross is that we find our life, our salvation, and our freedom in Christ alone. Everything else is secondary. His mercy is freely offered to all. There are no restrictions on who can come to him. Christ has never been exclusive or demanding with his love. He is our salvation and our hope. He is our fulfillment and our source.

Any requirements outside of Christ, including constantly seeking the miraculous or whatever leads us to success in the eyes of the world, are meaningless. They do not lead us to a deeper knowledge of God. They lead us to find fulfillment outside of Christ, but Christ is our heavenly leader and the true King. Let us look to his wisdom above all.

Jesus, you are my Savior and my King. I follow you and your kingdom ways. I choose to align in your love even when it looks like foolishness to those who are constantly looking for satisfaction in comfort or the next great thing. I believe that your ways are better.

KEEP BUILDING UP

Encourage one another and build one another up,
just as you are doing.

1 THESSALONIANS 5:11 ESV

Every day is an opportunity to encourage someone. Every moment is an opportunity to receive encouragement. May we not get so distracted by our to-do lists that we forget how important it is to connect with each other in meaningful ways.

When was the last time you intentionally built someone up with a word of encouragement, a smile, or a helping hand? Today, may you take every opportunity you find to meet someone with kindness. May you be a ray of sunshine on someone else's cloudy day. Remember what has been helpful for you on your own gray days and pay it forward. Every movement in love is significant; not one is overlooked by God.

Jesus, thank you for the power of encouragement in our lives. Encourage me in your Word and through others today as I reach out to give the same to others.

HE SHINES THROUGH

We now have this light shining in our hearts, but we ourselves are like fragile clay jars containing this great treasure. This makes it clear that our great power is from God, not from ourselves.

2 CORINTHIANS 4:7 NLT

No matter how broken you feel, remember that God's light shines from within. It doesn't matter how fragile your vessel is, Christ shines through every crack. His lifegiving light is your strength and source, and it shines through for others to see.

May you turn to face Jesus today and fill up on his presence. Spend time in his Word and meditate on his truth that sets you free. If you have a song, sing it freely. If you have a prayer, pray it boldly. If you have an act of kindness to offer, do it with compassion. He is shining through every movement of surrender to his love.

Jesus, I want your light to shine in my heart and purify my motives, my thoughts, and my choices. Thank you for your power at work in my life through your mercy. Even when I feel I have nothing to offer, I have your fullness.

OCTOBER

The Lord is good,
a refuge in times of trouble.
He cares for those who trust in him.

Nahum 1:7 niv

KNOWING HIM

By his divine power, God has given us everything we need for living a godly life. We have received all of this by coming to know him, the one who called us to himself by means of his marvelous glory and excellence.

2 PETER 1:3 NLT

Knowing Jesus is the greatest way to grow in wisdom, in love, and in integrity. It is through fellowship with him through his Spirit that we get to know what he is like more and more. When you spend time with someone, you get to know the inflection of that voice. You pick up unique mannerisms. When you spend time with Jesus, you will get to know the tone and feeling of his voice as well as what he says.

Through Christ, you have all you need for living a godly life. You will not find a better example of surrendered living than Christ to the Father. His kingdom is abundant and full of everything you require. His love will be your strength, his grace will be the power that enables you to persevere, and his joy will be your fuel for living. No one can take away his peace. Whatever you need, find it in his presence today.

Jesus, it is my honor to spend my life knowing you. I give you my time and attention. I offer you my heart and my mind. Teach me, fellowship with me, and lead me.

ONE THING

One thing I ask from the LORD, this only do I seek:
that I may dwell in the house of the LORD
all the days of my life, to gaze on the beauty of the LORD
and to seek him in his temple.

PSALM 27:4 NIV

Have you ever spent a perfect day with someone you love? Where everything you did felt more meaningful, no matter how mundane, because it was with them? In Psalm 84, the psalmist writes, "Better is one day in your courts than a thousand elsewhere." Better is one day spent in the presence of God than a thousand spent on your own.

May you know the all-surpassing goodness of God's presence in this way. May you long for him the way David longed for the presence of the Lord. May you find the satisfaction the psalmist found in the courts of his King.

Jesus, you are the one thing I look for. You are the one thing sustaining me. You are the one thing that fills me with inexpressible joy and pleasure. You are the one thing.

HOLY VISION

I don't depend on my own strength to accomplish this;
however I do have one compelling focus: I forget all of
the past as I fasten my heart to the future instead.

PHILIPPIANS 3:13 TPT

In the verse leading up to the one we are focusing on
today, Paul was clear that he had not yet acquired the
fullness he was pursuing. He also said that he was running
with passion into God's abundance (3:12). Paul was a
pursuer of God as much as God was a pursuer of Paul. May
we be encouraged to keep pressing into Christ Jesus in the
same way.

It is not our strength that gets us to where we want to go.
God's grace empowers and helps us move toward his love.
Let's let go of the regrets of yesterday and fix our eyes on
Jesus as the prize of our lives. He is better than we know.
He is full of more than we can imagine delighting in. His
kingdom is our goal, and it's our focus. Let's keep our eyes
focused on him.

*Jesus, you are holy, and you are my vision. I don't know
what tomorrow will bring, but I know you will be with me
until the end. You won't ever let up in love, and you won't
let me go. Hallelujah!*

LIFEGIVING PATH

You make known to me the path of life;
you will fill me with joy in your presence,
with eternal pleasures at your right hand.

PSALM 16:11 NIV

Are you struggling with direction? Do you need some help deciding where to go from here? Let Jesus be your advisor, for he is full of abundant wisdom. It is pure, and it is for your benefit. Even as you choose, know that you have freedom. He will be with you wherever you go. When you go, he will continue to guide you into his goodness.

The path of life is found through Jesus. His path is marked by laid-down love, and it does not cater to or coddle us. It both challenges and refines us. Even so, there is great joy in his presence. His help is always near. He leads us to his kingdom with mercy. He will continue to do this.

Jesus, I look to you for direction and wisdom. I trust you will help me no matter where my steps take me. Direct my path even as I walk it. I trust you to lead me.

ENDURING HOPE

Be joyful because you have hope.
Be patient when trouble comes,
and pray at all times.

ROMANS 12:12 NCV

In Christ, we always have hope. There is not a moment we are without it. Even when the blackness of night clouds our vision, Christ is constant. His light still shines. We can trust him to continue to guide us. We can trust his leadership and his care of us.

When troubles come, may we be patient and hold on to hope. As we keep praying at all times, our souls will be strengthened in his fellowship from Spirit to spirit. Our hearts will know the encouragement of his never-ending love as we continue to rely on him. He is our hope, and our hope will never fail.

Jesus, I take joy in your presence now. You are so very near. It doesn't matter what happens or doesn't happen in my life; you sustain me with your peace, joy, love, and hope. I won't stop praying. Thank you for hearing me.

CALM IN HIS PRESENCE

When the cares of my heart are many,
your consolations cheer my soul.

PSALM 94:19 ESV

When our thoughts spin out of control with anxiety, may we tune in to God's close presence. We can turn our attention to his nearness. We are never alone. When our burdens weigh us down, let's remember we don't have to carry them alone.

In the comfort of Christ's presence, there is not only solace; there is joy too. When we are relieved of our anxiety in his soothing peace, there is space to receive the delight of his love. Whenever we find ourselves overwhelmed by life's troubles, may we be calmed by the presence of the Spirit who breathes life, peace, joy, and hope into our hearts. In his love, we see more clearly.

Jesus, your love is better than any I've known. You lift the burdens of my heart and bring clarity to my confusion. You bring peace and rest. You calm and soothe my heart in your merciful embrace. Do it again, Lord, and may I be filled with your delight once more.

NEVER FORGET

"Teach them to faithfully follow all that I have commanded you. And never forget that I am with you every day, even to the completion of this age."

MATTHEW 28:20 TPT

When Jesus instructed his disciples to go out and make more disciples by spreading the good news of the kingdom of God, he encouraged them in a couple of ways. First, he instructed them to teach their own disciples to faithfully follow his words and teachings. He also encouraged them to remember his presence with them.

Jesus was not being philosophical about this reminder. He meant that every day he would be with them. It would not in the way they were accustomed to, but he would be there through the Holy Spirit. He promised he would never leave them, and this is true for us, too. Never forget, beloved, that Christ is with you every day.

Jesus, thank you for the promise of your presence every day. Reveal yourself to me in new ways and continue to lead me in your truth. I choose to align my life with your teachings, and I depend on your presence as my help and guide.

SIMPLY REMAIN

"I am the vine; you are the branches.
If you remain in me and I in you,
you will bear much fruit;
apart from me you can do nothing."

JOHN 15:5 NIV

Living in a self-reliant age, it is easy to forget how reliant we are on Christ and his work in us to produce spiritual fruit. Though we get to work and partner with him, it is his life in ours that produces the fruit of his kingdom. We do not need to strive to earn his love, and we do not need to push ourselves to the breaking point to reap his harvest.

Jesus is our true vine. We are the branches. The Father prunes us to help us grow and produce fruit. Let's not forget to remain in Christ. Have we gone our own way and added to the requirements he set forth? Do we have unrealistic standards of ourselves and others? Let's take the opportunity to simplify today and get back to the main goal: to remain connected to Christ.

Jesus, thank you for the work you do in the world and in my life. I trust you to produce kingdom fruit in my life as I learn to rest in you. When pruning comes, may I simply remain and trust your process.

A FRUITFUL LIFE

Who is wise and understanding among you?
By his good conduct let him show his works
in the meekness of wisdom.

JAMES 3:13 ESV

The wisdom of God does not shout or push people away. It invites us into the love of God with gentleness and humility. What kind of wisdom are we displaying in our lives? Are we living according to Christ's merciful understanding or by the harsh standards of the world?

When we live aligned in the love of God, his peace, joy, and patience are evident. The fruit of endurance, compassion, and open-hearted surrender to the ways of Christ will be on display for all to see. Let's first focus on the gardens of our own hearts before we jump to judgment of others. Godly wisdom is full of humility, kindness, service to the greater good, and the truth of Jesus.

Jesus, I don't want to be full of earthly wisdom that is not based in you. I look to your example, your teachings, and your life to find the living expression of true wisdom. May my life reflect your values.

NO REASON TO FEAR

The Lord is my light and my salvation;
whom shall I fear?
The Lord is the stronghold of my life;
of whom shall I be afraid?

PSALM 27:1 ESV

When Jesus is our light and salvation, why should we fear what humans can do to us? With the Lord at the helm of our lives, holding us securely in his merciful love, why would we let fear direct our steps? There is no reason to fear even when we walk through dark nights of the soul. Christ is with us. He is our Savior, and he will not let us go.

When fear is in the driver's seat, it will try to steer us away from pain. It might keep us stuck in cycles of shame. It may turn us back to things we had left behind. We are not victims to fear. Christ has liberated us in his love, and his perfect love drives out fear. Let's rise up in our agency and refuse to let fear lead us when love is our Shepherd.

Jesus, I don't want to live under fear's leadership in my life. I refuse to do it any longer. I trust your heart and your wisdom. I will follow you as you lead me in calm and steady steps.

HIGHER VISION

We set our eyes not on what we see but on what we cannot see. What we see will last only a short time, but what we cannot see will last forever.

2 Corinthians 4:18 NCV

The kingdom of God cannot be seen by the naked eye. It is not found in some far-off land or in one particular church or people of faith. It isn't found in a nation, and it is not in the governments of this world. One day, we will live in the physical realm of his kingdom, but right now we live in this present age, and this world will one day pass away.

May Jesus, who we cannot see but still know, be our vision. His Spirit is with us. We catch glimpses of his glorious kingdom through the fruit of his mercy in our lives. He moves in miracles, and he calms us with his peace. His presence is tangible, and it is always with us.

Jesus, the ways of your kingdom are mysterious and yet so real. I turn my attention to you and use my imagination to focus on your love, goodness, and mercy. I look to you with my mind, and I focus on the wonderful truth of who you are.

WORDS TO LIVE BY

Warn those who are lazy.
Encourage those who are timid.
Take tender care of those who are weak.
Be patient with everyone.

1 Thessalonians 5:14 NLT

Words of encouragement are a balm to our souls and provide courage when we need it. A well-spoken word at the right time can redirect and align us. With kindness, we can encourage those who feel inadequate by reminding them that God is with them. He will be their strength. When we see the weak, and we will all be weak at different times, we should take care of them and lift them up instead of passing them by.

In the parable of the Good Samaritan, Jesus illustrates that when we care for others without bias, we are extending the love of the Father. When we demonstrate kindness and mercy, we walk in the light of Christ's love. Let's look for ways to do that today through encouragement and care.

Jesus, you are the greatest encourager. I am built up on your loving words, and your truth is my foundation. Help me to be a lifter of other's hearts, bodies, and souls, just as you are to all who look to you.

THERE IS A LIGHT

A light shines in the dark for honest people,
for those who are merciful and kind and good.

PSALM 112:4 NCV

When we live with open and gracious hearts that are tender, kind, and true, we can rest assured that the brilliant light of Christ will shine through even our darkest nights. With integrity as our value system, the kingdom of God is amplified. No matter what we face, let's keep living as the vessels of God's mercy.

As we continue to choose generosity and compassion, Christ continues to shine through us. Our confidence is in Christ and in his faithfulness. It is not in what we do. Still, we choose to live for him because his love is incomparable. May you see the light of his presence shining brightly today. May you be the light of his presence to others.

Jesus, thank you for your constant presence of lifegiving light. I choose to live for your kingdom and in line with your ways. I choose compassion over self-protection, mercy over judgment, and kindness over apathy. You are my light and my strength.

OPEN DOOR

"I am the door. If anyone enters by me, he will be saved and will go in and out and find pasture."

JOHN 10:9 ESV

Jesus is the door into life, freedom, and soul-satisfaction. Only through him do we find the rest we are searching for. He is full of peace, tender care, and sharp truth that separates marrow and bone.

Jesus is our Good Shepherd. He leads us into fields of plenty. He guides us into lush pastures and leads us beside still waters where we can be refreshed and restored. He is our peace and our life; he is our salvation. When we enter through him, on his invitation, we find all we are looking for and more than we can expect. He is better than we can imagine.

Jesus, you alone are the Good Shepherd. I trust you with my life. My heart is yours, and I follow you. May I always be able to recognize your voice and distinguish between your truth and the lies of wolves. I trust you.

EMPOWERING FAITH

Faith empowers us to see that the universe
was created and beautifully coordinated
by the power of God's words! He spoke and
the invisible realm gave birth to all that is seen.

HEBREWS 11:3 TPT

Today's verse come from the often-called faith chapter of
Hebrews. Here, we are reminded of the fruit of the faith
from those who have gone before. We don't have to worry
about whether or not faith is empowering us if we are
aligning our lives in Christ. It is all seeds of Christ's work
within us. We get to choose what seeds get watered, so
let's tend to our hearts with intention.

The universe, and all that is within it, is the handiwork of
our Creator. He spoke, and what did not exist came into
being. There are no accidents in creation. It is wonderfully
designed, intricately coordinated, and marvelously
connected. Let's take time outside to notice the patterns
playing out in beautiful ways, and may our faith grow in the
wonder of it all.

*Jesus, your faithfulness is stronger than my faith, and I am
so grateful for that. Thank you for the leaves that change
and fall, for the shifting of seasons, and for the glory of
the stars in the sky. Awaken my heart in awe and wonder
as I consider your creation.*

BE STILL

"The Lord will fight for you,
you have only to be still."

Exodus 14:14 NIV

There are some battles we have to fight in this life. Work is not something we will only experience in this life either. However, there is a difference between partnering with God in what we do and surviving a battle we are ill-equipped to win.

There will be times when God fights our battles for us. When the odds are against us, when others slander our names and character without reason, when we are up against impossible factors that are out of our control, let's lean into the presence of God with us. He is Emmanuel. He is Yahweh. He is powerful to save. If you find yourself in an impossible situation, be still in God's presence and let him fight for you.

Jesus, I trust that when you say rest, you mean it. I also trust that when I need to move, you will direct me. For now, I rest in your presence and take courage and strength in your faithfulness. Fight the battles I can't win, Lord.

SPILLING OVER

I spill out my heart to you
and tell you all my troubles.

PSALM 142:2 TPT

Whatever is in your heart today, spill it out to the Lord. Tell him your cares and your troubles. Don't hold anything back. He cares for you. When you are desperate, overwhelmed, and about to give up, look to the Lord for help, and he will show you the way to go.

The Lord is your hiding place, and he will not abandon you. Cry out to him in your distress and pour out your praises in your celebration. Wherever you are, whatever you are facing, bring it all before the Lord. He can handle your messy emotions. He can read your heart even when you have no words. Trust him, rely on him, and don't stop running to him.

Jesus, I know I don't have to run far to find you. You are so very close and so very real to me. I spill my heart out to you today. Meet me here and love me to life in your presence.

GOOD REWARD

Remember that the Lord will reward each one of us
for the good we do.

EPHESIANS 6:8 NLT

In this chapter in Ephesians, Paul addresses how we are
to love in our families and workplaces. The context of this
verse specifically is in regard to our work ethic. Whatever
good we do in our jobs, the Lord will reward us for. When
we work with integrity, he takes notice, and so do others.
No matter what our title or job description, how we work
matters.

May we take our work seriously and do what is right at
all times. Let's not look for ways to get out of work, but
let's do all before us with ingenuity, a good work ethic,
and integrity. It is pleasing to Christ when we serve those
we work with and for as if we are serving him. May we be
people who do the right thing at all times whether others
are watching or not. We know Christ sees all.

*Jesus, I needed this reminder today. I will keep choosing
to work with integrity and honor because you are worth it.
I do it for you first!*

KEEPING ON

Never become tired of doing good.

2 Thessalonians 3:13 NCV

Did you know your work can be a form of worship? How you approach what you do, day in and day out, reflects your values. When you are honest by following through on your commitments and setting appropriate boundaries around your work, you can be confident in your offering before the Lord.

As you live your life as a living sacrifice before the Lord, there are times when you will be motivated in love and other times when you are weary. Keep pressing on in the good that is yours to do. Incorporate rhythms of rest into your schedule just as God exemplified. Every day is a new opportunity to press in and press on. There will be a plentiful harvest in the end.

Jesus, you are my strength, my support, and my vision. When I grow tired, empower me by your grace to keep choosing to do good. May my life be a pleasing fragrance of worship before you.

ALL DAY LONG

Lead me by your truth and teach me,
for you are the God who saves me.
All day long I put my hope in you.

PSALM 25:5 NLT

How different would your inner world look if you consciously chose to put your hope in God all day long? Have you up against an unforeseen problem? Thank God for his help, put your hope in him, and get some counsel. Devastated by the bad reports flooding the news? Pray for those affected, put your hope in him, help where you can, and take a break from media.

There are as many ways to practice putting our hope in God as there are people in this world. May we not grow tired in trusting him, for he is faithful. May we not grow weary of relying on his help, for he will never change in loyal love. All day long, let's put our hope in him.

Jesus, help me to choose to put my active trust in you again and again as I go throughout my day. Turn my attention to you when I am distracted and remind me of your faithful goodness and power to save.

SPIRIT POWER

God gave us a spirit not of fear
but of power and love and self-control.

2 Timothy 1:7 esv

Jesus is the light of the world. There are no shadows of fear in him. He is pure, radiant light. He is pure, radiant love. 1 John 4:16 says, "God is love, and whoever abides in love abides in God, and God abides in him." A couple verses later, it continues, "There is no fear in love, but perfect love casts out fear." In Christ, we are not awaiting punishment; we are living in freedom. "Fear," John says, "has to do with punishment, and whoever fears has not been perfected in love" (verse 18).

We have been given the Spirit who is full of powerful love. May we live in the liberty of Christ's mercy and not be bound again to the fear from which he set us free.

Jesus, thank you for your Spirit. Where fear seeks to restrict, you have torn down walls to expand in love. I am so grateful that you are better than the leaders of this world who seek to control through fear. I am grounded, and I grow on the foundation of your love.

IN HIS NAME

Our help is in the name of the Lord,
the Maker of heaven and earth.

PSALM 124:8 NIV

In the name of Jesus, we have our help. Proverbs 18:10 declares, "The name of the Lord is a fortified tower; the righteous run to it and are safe." When we don't know where else to turn, our Savior is a refuge and hiding place. May we never stop calling on his name.

The name of the Lord is power. In John 14, Jesus said, "I will do whatever you ask in my name, so that the Father may be glorified in the Son. You may ask for anything in my name, and I will do it." The name of Jesus isn't a party trick or some mystic mantra. We call upon the person of Jesus to intervene in our lives and in the world, and he responds. He is that good.

Jesus, I'm grateful to know you through fellowship with your Spirit. Encourage me today as I call on you and pray in your name. Your powerful love is incomparable, and I won't stop pressing in to know you more.

FREEDOM IS HERE

The Lord is the Spirit,
and wherever the Spirit of the Lord is,
there is freedom.

2 CORINTHIANS 3:17 NLT

Only through Christ can we understand the kingdom of God clearly. It is through his Spirit that we are set free to know him, follow him, and be transformed in his glory. There is no better time to look to him than now. There is no better moment than the present.

Where in your life do you have the freedom of Christ's love shining through? Where do you want more freedom? The Spirit of the Lord is with you, and by the Spirit's power, you are liberated. May you experience a deeper liberty in his love than you have yet known. There is always more wisdom to find, more mercy to expand our understanding, and more freedom to choose our way.

Jesus, I trust you as my leader and friend. I am indebted to you as my Savior and Redeemer. I won't stop looking to you, and I know you are not finished working your power in my life.

ASTONISHING FAITHFULNESS

Your love is so extravagant it reaches to the heavens,
Your faithfulness so astonishing it stretches to the sky!

PSALM 57:10 TPT

Have you ever been astonished by God's faithfulness?
Perhaps you have walked with someone through drawn-
out periods of waiting and were able to witness their
breakthrough. Perhaps you have experienced a miracle of
God's mercy in your life.

Spend some time in the Word and in reading the
testimonies of those who have experienced the delight of
God's fulfilled promises. Let it increase your faith in areas
where you are still waiting for change to come. May you be
encouraged in the presence of God as you marvel at how
extravagantly good his love is toward all who trust in him.

*Jesus, I look to you. I trust you. I have tasted and seen
your goodness, and I am longing for more. Increase my
faith as I reflect on your faithfulness to others. Open my
eyes to see where you have met me with your mercy time
and again. I worship you!*

LOVING ACTION

Little children, let us love,
not in word or speech,
but in truth and action.

1 JOHN 3:18 NRSV

Love is not love that does not follow through on its intentions. If we claim to love Christ and want to live like him, our lives will show it. When we show kindness and compassion, we reflect the love of God alive in us. When we promote peace and practice mercy in tangible ways, we show that love is a value that we not only claim but also live by.

Think about who you see on a regular basis. Who do you interact with daily? Do they know you as a person of love? Have they witnessed compassion in action through you? If you need a refresher of what love looks like, you can look to Jesus, and you can also spend time in 1 Corinthians 13. May you be a person who practices what she preaches.

Jesus, your love is not just a feeling; it is so much more. It is active, it is lived out, and it is a practice. I don't want to say one thing and then live my life differently. Show me where love is absent in my life and help me actively choose it in my relationships.

RUN TO WIN

Do you not know that in a race the runners all compete,
but only one receives the prize?
Run in such a way that you may win it.

1 CORINTHIANS 9:24 NRSV

Though our lives are not at competition with others, we can train in excellence to run the race set before us. The race of life is not won by taking others out along the way; it is achieved by relying on the grace and strength of Jesus, keeping our vision on him, and leaning on others for help when we need it.

Do you know what you are building in your life? Are there goals you are training to reach or places you are looking to go? Our ambitions can be as simple as loving those around us well or leaving a legacy of wisdom to those who come after us. Let's remember what Christ said when he summed up the law in one statement: "In everything, do to others as you would have them do to you" (Matthew 7:12). What a necessary guidepost that is in this race of life.

Jesus, thank you for your simple wisdom. I want to run the race of this life with endurance and to lean on your grace for strength and understanding when I run out. You are my vision.

FAITH THAT PLEASES

Without faith living within us it would be impossible to please God. For we come to God in faith knowing that he is real and that he rewards the faith of those who passionately seek him.

HEBREWS 11:6 TPT

When we know how intricately we are known, how thoroughly we are accepted, and how completely we are loved by God, our faith grows stronger. In Christ, all our shame and sin has been completely covered. His mercy is strong; it purifies, strengthens, and transforms us.

May you find your faith growing stronger as you press in to know the truth of who Jesus is, his lasting legacy, and what life looks like in him. His kingdom cannot be shaken, and every vow he has made will be fulfilled. He is easy to please, so keep passionately pursuing him.

Jesus, you are the joy of my life. You are the source of my faith. Breathe on my heart and let hope arise in new ways today. I look to you, Lord.

SUBMITTED TO GOD

Submit yourselves, then, to God.
Resist the devil, and he will flee from you.

JAMES 4:7 NIV

In order to get a clearer understanding of what James was talking about when submitting to God, it's important to look at the preceding verses. He was addressing a people who fought each other because of envy. They were looking to satisfy their pleasures by whatever means necessary. James rebuked them, but he also reminded them of God's abundant grace: "He gives us more grace. Scripture says: 'God opposes the proud but shows favor to the humble'" (James 4:6).

What is the way of humility? To submit ourselves to God. That is always the first step. When we are submitted to Christ, we can resist the temptations of this world. If we want to live in the true liberty of Christ's love, we will submit to him. Freedom comes from living in the light of his mercy.

Jesus, you are my Savior. I submit my life to you. I will rely on your power at work within me to empower me to live with integrity, mercy, and peace. Thank you.

INFINITE UNDERSTANDING

How great is our God!
There's absolutely nothing
his power cannot accomplish,
and he has infinite understanding of everything.

PSALM 147:5 TPT

In a world where we are constantly discovering more about the universe and how it works, we know there is more mystery than understanding in our midst. However, nothing is a mystery to God. Nothing surprises him. He is full of infinite understanding about everything.

It is our joy, then, to grow and increase in the knowledge of Jesus whose wisdom knows no limits. His power is able to do much more than we can even imagine. Let's give ourselves to knowing Christ more and more. Let's fellowship with him through every trial and victory, every hill and valley of this life. He is so very great, and he is so very near.

Jesus, when I can't see my way out of my confusion, you lead me with your peace. I want to know you more today. Reveal your incomparable wisdom in new ways to my mind, heart, and life. I love you, and it is my honor to know you.

GENUINE AFFECTION

Love each other with genuine affection
and take delight in honoring each other.

ROMANS 12:10 NLT

Love cannot be faked. It is not something we have to wait
to experience either. We get to choose to extend mercy
to others, not out of obligation, but out of a heart that has
known such mercy received. Do you need a fresh touch of
God's love? Do you need a reminder of how strong it is?
Turn to Jesus today for help. He will give it.

Think of who you are genuinely affectionate toward.
You probably have at least a few. Now, consider the
compassion of Christ that reaches toward you with genuine
affection. He loves you because he loves you. When you
are full of this love, you have the same compassion to offer
others. May you choose to love others by delighting in and
honoring those you get to do life with.

*Jesus, I know that as I experience your genuine affection,
I have an overflowing source of kindness to offer others.
Fill me up today until your love is my source of strength,
mercy, and courage. Thank you.*

FILLED UP

Fill us with your love every morning.
Then we will sing and rejoice all our lives.

PSALM 90:14 NCV

The love of God is strong and sure. It is always reaching toward us, and it is eternally abundant. There is no lack of mercy in the heart of our good Father. Through Christ, we have unhindered fellowship with him. Every morning, every day, every moment, there is more love to receive.

When we are filled with the love of God, there is always reason to sing and rejoice. He never lets us go. Even when we walk through dark valleys of sorrow, rejoicing is promised to come again in the light of the morning. When we are traveling through dark nights of the soul, the love of Christ is abundant and clear even there. May we know the all-surpassing goodness of his affection and rejoice in his love all the days of our lives.

Jesus, there is no one like you! You do not change with the seasons or with the news of the day. You are not swayed by politics or by pessimists. You are eternally strong, forever faithful, and always abounding in love. I rejoice in your love.

NOVEMBER

Because of the LORD's great love
we are not consumed,
for his compassions never fail.
They are new every morning;
great is your faithfulness.

LAMENTATIONS 3:22-23 NIV

SECRET PRAYERS

"When you pray, go into your room, close the door and pray to your Father, who is unseen. Then your Father, who sees what is done in secret, will reward you."

MATTHEW 6:6 NIV

Not every prayer we pray needs to be broadcast or shared with others. The Lord knows our vulnerability and our hopes. He knows our greatest struggles and pleas. There is no need to share our most sacred prayers or holiest hopes with any who would listen. These are things that should only be shared with our most trusted confidants.

We do not owe anyone the information that is between us and the Lord. This is not to say that there isn't a place for confession, bearing each other's burdens, or vulnerability with trusted friends. However, we should be wary of those who demand to know more than we are comfortable sharing. Instead, let's pray first to our Father. Let's bare our hearts and lives to him as a living prayer. Then, we can be wise about who else gets the privilege of knowing our hearts.

Jesus, I look to your example. You found time to sneak away with the Father and pray privately with him. You are the foundation of my day and the place where I pour everything out. I trust that you are enough. You will give me wisdom on when, where, and with whom to share pieces of my heart.

TRUST AND BELIEVE

"Don't worry or surrender to your fear. For you've believed in God, now trust and believe in me also."

JOHN 14:1 TPT

Before he spoke these words, Jesus shared with his disciples that he wouldn't be with them for much longer. He told them that they, who had followed him for three years, could not go with him. This must have been a shock to the disciples. They had followed Jesus, lived with him, and learned from him. He was their teacher, yet he was preparing for what lay ahead on the cross.

Even so, Jesus comforted his friends. He told them to not worry or surrender to their fear. Fear shuts us down and takes over our nervous systems, but Jesus is our peace. He has a place for us in his Father's kingdom just as he does for his disciples. Even then, he knew what lay ahead of him and his followers. He knows what lays ahead of us now. Trust him and keep trusting. Don't worry or surrender to your fear. His Spirit goes with you into every sphere.

Jesus, I will not give in to my worry today. I lay it at your feet, and I surrender my fear to your peace. I believe you are the way, the truth, and the life. Empower me with the grace of your presence as I continue to walk with you.

DIVINE UNITY

I appeal to you, brothers and sisters, in the name of our Lord Jesus Christ, that all of you agree with one another in what you say and that there be no divisions among you, but that you be perfectly united in mind and thought.

1 CORINTHIANS 1:10 NIV

Paul was addressing specific divisions in the church at Corinth in this passage. They were divided over which apostle they were following, over their socio-economic status, and over spiritual gifts. They were so distracted by these issues it was taking away from the message of Christ. Paul appealed to the Corinthian church to be united around the love of Christ.

Our highest aim and ambition is to love each other well. It is not difficult to pinpoint areas of division in our churches either. There seems to be an overabundance of opinions that keep us fighting over insubstantial issues. Still, the call to love God and each other well is the main call. Where we have become distracted and divided, let's focus once more on what Christ taught: love. Love is the only force strong enough to unite us.

Jesus, forgive me for times I have become distracted by issues that divide your people. I want to choose love above all else.

SUIT UP

Put on God's complete set of armor provided for us, so that you will be protected as you fight against the evil strategies of the accuser!

EPHESIANS 6:11 TPT

The armor of God is ours through Christ. Through our fellowship and union with Jesus, we have access to all the supernatural strength we need. He is our victory, and our lives are conduits of his power.

When was the last time you considered the significance of the armor of God? Today, may you intentionally put on the belt of truth and the breastplate of righteousness to protect your heart. Make your feet ready to move with the gospel of peace. Use faith as your shield against the fiery darts of the evil one. Put on the helmet of salvation to protect your thoughts from lies. Lastly, take the sharp Spirit-sword of the Word of God. As you read through the rest of the chapter, consider how this armor protects and readies you for living victoriously in Christ.

Jesus, thank you for fellowship with you above all. I will put on the full armor you offer and trust that you will guide me through the battles of this life. Thank you.

EVIDENCE OF THE UNSEEN

Faith shows the reality of what we hope for;
it is the evidence of things we cannot see.

HEBREWS 11:1 NLT

May you be encouraged to keep persevering in faith today
as you look to Christ. If you have a few minutes to spare,
read through the whole of Hebrews 11. What evidence of
faith do you recognize in your own life, community, and in
the world?

Faith is not fragile. It holds on through droughts and
storms alike. It keeps persevering through trials and
failures. The love of God never lets go, and the mercy of
God works through the pitfalls of our stories. God is faithful
to do everything he promised he would, so let's keep
pressing on in faith. Let's not give up hope, for the one
who has called us, guides us, and redeems us is faithful and
true. He will never fail.

*Jesus, thank you for the power of your loyal love. As I
look for the evidence of your faithfulness in and around
me, give me eyes to see where you have been working
all along. You are great, and I trust that you are still the
restorer of broken and lost things.*

THE FINAL WORD

"No one can undo what I have done."

ISAIAH 43:13 NLT

The Lord is purposeful in all he does. He does not waver in his decisions, and once he chooses to act, no one can reverse it. He is infinite in mercy and power that brings life out of desolate places. He is the final say. When he chooses someone as his own, no one can talk him out of his love.

Beloved, do you know that in Christ, you have freedom of fellowship with the Father? He has chosen you, and you are his. Do not hesitate in self-doubt or shame. Come to him, for he welcomes you with open arms. Jesus paved the way to the Father through his death and resurrection. His love, which is incomparable, cannot be overstated. The power of his resurrection is our life and strength. No one can undo the power of his sacrifice. He has the final word over everything; that includes our very lives.

Jesus, you are my Savior. I cannot begin to express gratitude for your resurrection life and the power of your love. Open my understanding to know you more in Spirit and in truth. I look to you.

FOUNTAIN OF LIFE

To know you is to experience a flowing fountain,
drinking in your life, springing up to satisfy.
In your light we receive the light of revelation.

PSALM 36:9 TPT

Does this description of fellowship with the Lord sound too good to be true? Does it sound a little "out-there" to your experience? If so, accept this dare: ask Jesus to reveal the goodness of his presence to you in this way today.

If you have known this feeling before but it feels distant to you now, be encouraged to press in for a fresh encounter with his overwhelming grace. His love is like a flowing fountain. It is always fresh, pure, and full of relief. We drink in his life, and it springs up within us to satisfy our souls. In the light of his presence, we receive the light of revelation. May all this and more be your experience as you spend time with the Lord today.

Jesus, I want to know the refreshing fountain of your life flowing within mine. Awaken my heart to your goodness, enliven my soul in your affection, and expand my understanding in your glorious wisdom.

TEST OF PATIENCE

You know that the testing of your faith
produces perseverance.

JAMES 1:3 NIV

We cannot escape times of testing in our lives. Unforeseen problems are part of the human experience, and we cannot control them. Still, we know God is with us. He is with us through it all. What a relief it is to know that God cannot be caught off-guard! His plans are never derailed.

When times of testing come, may you press in to know the presence of God with you. He will strengthen you to keep going. He will produce patience and perseverance in your heart as you lean on him. His help is always near. There is nothing lacking for those who learn to lean on the help of Jesus in all things. His grace is more than enough to empower you in your weakness.

Jesus, I wish life was easier. However, you didn't promise a perfect and comfortable life to those who follow you. You did promise to never abandon us. Thank you. Be my strength, my hope, and my song forever.

CHOSEN

"You did not choose me; I chose you.
And I gave you this work:
to go and produce fruit, fruit that will last.
Then the Father will give you
anything you ask for in my name."

JOHN 15:16 NCV

Read this verse again. Instead of picturing Jesus speaking to his disciples, visualize him speaking directly to you here and now. Before you even knew to choose him, he chose you. You are not an afterthought, and you did not somehow sneak your way into his kingdom.

He knows you through and through, and he has given you work to do. It is to produce fruit in your life. How do you do that? By abiding in him. As you grow to know Christ more and more, you will know what his voice sounds like. You will know which way to go when you are at a fork in the road. You will know the greatest call over your life is to love. You will produce the Spirit's fruit of his kingdom as you lean on him in all things.

Jesus, thank you for choosing me. Thank you for loving me to life. I know everything that is worthwhile and beautiful is from you. I want to know you more.

HIGHER TRUST

"People everywhere seem to worry about making a living, but your heavenly Father knows your every need and will take care of you."

LUKE 12:30 TPT

It can be difficult not to get caught up in the passions and opinions of others when they are shared so frequently. We live in an age when we can see what people around the world are doing just by looking at our phones. Now more than ever, we are inundated with calls to be better, do better, and fight for numerous causes.

While it is good to be challenged, let's not lose sight of our own lanes. What has God called us to? Where has he planted us? Who are we already in relationship with? Can we put effort into loving more, encouraging each other, and trusting that God will take care of us? He knows our specific and specialized needs, and he will not fail us. Let's focus on our own lives, our own gardens, and the people we interact with. He will take care of the rest.

Jesus, thank you for the goodness of your care. I trust you to provide for me. I trust you to continue to guide me in your clarifying wisdom. Help me to not worry about where I think I should be and instead trust you in all things.

FAITHFUL MERCY

Do not, O LORD, withhold your mercy from me;
let your steadfast love and your faithfulness
keep me safe forever.

PSALM 40:11 NRSV

Jesus did not withhold mercy from those whom others were quick to judge. In John 8, the religious leaders brought an adulteress before him. They wanted to trap him by getting him to break the laws of Moses. The law in question was that a woman in this position should be stoned.

Jesus' response was to ask a sinless person to throw the first stone. Then, he wrote in the dust with his hand. We do not know what he wrote or drew, but all the woman's accusers eventually left. The Word says that they left convicted, so the confronting truth got to them. In the end, there was no one left to condemn this woman, and Jesus blessed her and mercifully told her to be free from a life of sin. This kind of mercy is what we find in Christ over and over again. It is beautiful, liberating, and powerful.

Jesus, you did not teach that we should condemn or judge others. You preached mercy, and you lived it out. I want my life to reflect the same liberating love.

MINDS OF MERCY

May the God who gives endurance and encouragement give you the same attitude of mind toward each other that Christ Jesus had.

ROMANS 15:5 NIV

The unity we are looking for is found first in our relationship with Jesus. None of us is more favored than the other. We are brothers and sisters who are offered the same blessings and resources of Christ's kingdom as any other.

May we look for ways to encourage one another as needed. May we offer mercy toward one another just as we hope to receive mercy from others. May we be kind, true, and full of love that endures hard seasons. What we long for, we are able to offer others. What Christ offers us we are able to share with others.

Jesus, you are my source. In fellowship with you, I discover what love really looks like. I don't want to harbor unforgiveness or hatred toward anyone. Help me to let go, choose love over judgment, and live a life of mercy.

FIRM FOUNDATION

"The rain came down, the streams rose, and the winds blew and beat against that house; yet it did not fall, because it had its foundation on the rock."

MATTHEW 7:25 NIV

What is the foundation of your life built upon? Jesus said that those who hear his teaching and apply it to their lives are like a wise man who built his house on an unmovable foundation. When rains came, floods rose, and fierce winds beat against his house, it stood firm.

When we align our lives in Christ, not only knowing what he taught but also applying it to our lives, we can live with the confidence of an unshakeable foundation. Though storms may come, they will not tear our lives down. Let's take Jesus at his word and follow him.

Jesus, you are the firm foundation my life is built upon. Your love is my base, and it will not be moved. As I continue to build my life upon you, may I trust in your faithful mercy to keep me firmly situated in your kingdom.

HEART OF GRATITUDE

The LORD is my strength and shield.
I trust him with all my heart.
He helps me, and my heart is filled with joy.
I burst out in songs of thanksgiving.

PSALM 28:7 NLT

How has the Lord helped you? How have you experienced his mercy in your life? Let your testimony of his goodness be the jumping off point of your gratitude today. When we practice thanksgiving and offer the Lord our praise for what he has already done, our hearts are built up in encouragement of his faithfulness.

May your trust in Christ's unfailing love grow stronger today. May his grip of grace be clear to you. He has not let you go, and he will not let you go. He surrounds you with loyal love, and he upholds you with the strength of his victory. Pour out the joy that rises within you and offer your praise freely.

Jesus, you are so very worthy of my praise. I'm thankful for how you have come through for me, and I expect you will continue in faithfulness all the days of my life. Here is my song of praise!

WATCH OUT

Look after each other so that none of you fails to receive the grace of God. Watch out that no poisonous root of bitterness grows up to trouble you, corrupting many.

HEBREWS 12:15 NLT

What a beautiful declaration weaves within this passage. The writer does not say, "Look after each other to micromanage how you live out your faith." He encourages the community to look after each other so that no one misses out on the revelation of God's grace. God's grace is what saves us and what empowers us to live for Christ. It is freely offered to all in the same abundant measure.

As we care for each other, let's encourage one another in the grace of God. Let's watch over our own hearts to be sure that no bitterness toward another grows there. Bitterness only causes trouble. Love covers a multitude of sins. Let's remember this within our relationships and communities.

Jesus, your ways are better than my own tendencies. Where I would let bitterness grow, you offer a better way. I align myself in your love even as I am confronted with areas within me that do not agree with your kingdom. Please, transform me in your love.

COME BOLDLY

Because of Christ and our faith in him, we can now come boldly and confidently into God's presence.

EPHESIANS 3:12 NLT

What does it look like to come boldly before the throne of God? As sons and daughters of the living God, we get to express ourselves fully and freely. Our confidence is in who God says we are and not in our own merit.

May you grow in the confidence of your identity as a child of God today. Christ has completely fulfilled the demands of the law, and you can come to the Father without hesitancy. Freely share what is on your heart with him, for he is a good father, and he delights in you. Even when what you share isn't happy, he is pleased with you. Don't hold a thing back from him, for he is your helper, advocate, and teacher.

Jesus, thank you for breaking down every hindrance between humanity and the Father. Thank you for choosing me, for covering me in your mercy, and for saving me. I come boldly today, and I expect to know God more because of what you have done.

COURAGE AND STRENGTH

All you who put your hope in the LORD
be strong and brave.

PSALM 31:24 NCV

Have you put your hope in the Lord? Be strong and brave as you press ahead in your plans. Have you put your trust in Christ? Take confidence in his leadership and help when you need it. You do not need to rid yourself of fear before you step. Push through it and continue to hope, trust, and believe that God is for you.

There will be times when you are not sure what God wants for you. In those times, remember who he is. What does the fruit of his kingdom look like? What do you already know to be true about him? As you walk in courage, trust that God will not let you down. He is faithful.

Jesus, you are my strength and courage. I put my hope in you and leave it there. I leave my trust with you, and I throw my anchor of hope into the sea of your unending love. I know you are with me even when I cannot sense it.

BE MINDFUL

"In the same way you judge others,
you will be judged,
and with the measure you use,
it will be measured to you."

MATTHEW 7:2 NIV

When we refuse to recognize our biases in our assessment of others, pride masquerades as righteousness. Jesus was not kidding when he said that we should love others the way we want to be loved. The same principle applies with our judgment. Do we want others to base their opinions of us off of things we disagree about?

In this passage of Scripture, Jesus was encouraging people not to judge others at all. Do we harshly criticize others but then let ourselves off the hook? Do we dehumanize those we disagree with while leaving room for our own mistakes? Hopefully, we take Jesus at his word and leave the judgment to God. He doesn't need our help; he sees every heart clearly. May we make it our priority to extend mercy instead of judgment.

Jesus, what a kick in the pants this reminder is. I confess I judge others more harshly than I want to be judged on similar things. I trust your mercy is strong enough for us all. Forgive me and give me awareness whenever I step outside of your loving ways.

GENEROUS LIVING

God is able to provide you with every blessing
in abundance, so that by always having enough
of everything, you may share abundantly in every
good work.

2 CORINTHIANS 9:8 NRSV

There is no shortage in God's kingdom. His grace is more
than enough, his love is overflowing, and his peace is
plentiful. May we live as reflections of the generosity of our
good Father. May we never feel the need to hoard what we
have instead of mercifully caring for those in need around us.

God is generous. He is always giving us more out of the
endless resources of his kingdom. Every blessing is a gift
from him. We don't need to store them up in fear that he'll
one day change his mind. We don't need to hold tightly
to things that don't serve us anymore either. May we
charitably and freely share with those who have less than
we do. May we offer our abundance as shared fruits to
build up our communities. We are meant to thrive together
and help each other.

*Jesus, I want to be generous in my living and in my
giving. Where I have gone off-track, bring me back into
alignment. Bless the work of my hands as I share what I
have with others.*

CHOSEN TREASURE

You are God's chosen treasure—priests who are kings,
a spiritual "nation" set apart as God's devoted ones. He
called you out of darkness to experience his marvelous
light, and now he claims you as his very own.

1 PETER 2:9 TPT

Every person who submits to Christ is a part of the
kingdom of God. We become priests and kings of his
kingdom and co-heirs with Christ. We are God's chosen
treasure as people who are set apart to devote ourselves
to him. We do not dwell in the darkness of sin, fear, or
shame any longer; we are alive in the light of Christ.

Take heart today in your identity as a child of God and a
priest of his heavenly kingdom. You are part of a greater
family of God which is larger than you can imagine. There
are people from every tribe, every language, every nation
united under the banner of the Lamb of God. May you
rejoice in your place in the family of God, and may you
connect with your brothers and sisters in Christ.

Jesus, what a wonderful reality it is that I am in a family of
believers as diverse as it comes. I love your creativity, and
I am honored to know you and to be known by you. May I
move in confidence and compassion today.

KEEP SEEKING

Seek more of his strength! Seek more of him!
Let's always be seeking the light of his face.

PSALM 105:4 TPT

Today is the day the Lord has made. Don't give up on the good you have to do. Don't quit seeking the Lord. He has not abandoned you, so don't give up before you experience your breakthrough. No matter what, keep seeking him.

As the psalmist encouraged, seek more of his strength when you are weak. When you don't know what else to do, seek more of him! When you are in the dark of confusion, suffering, or grief, always be seeking the light of his face. For every moment, there is a reason to seek him. He is better than life itself, and he will satisfy your soul's deepest longings.

Jesus, I give you the sacrifice of my praise even when I don't feel like it. I seek after you when I would rather check out. I rely on you in everything, so don't let me down, Lord. I will keep persevering to know you more and more.

HE IS ABLE

He is able, once and forever, to save those who come to God through him. He lives forever to intercede with God on their behalf.

HEBREWS 7:25 NLT

When Jesus rose from the grave where he was buried, he broke the power of sin and death. When he ascended to the Father, he became, and still is, our great high priest. He continually intercedes for us before the Father. What a wonderful Savior he is!

Jesus is not at a loss for anyone who comes to him for help. He is able to save everyone who comes to God through him. He is holy without any hint of evil and unable to deceive or tell a lie. He is incapable of sinning, and he is highly exalted above the heavens (Hebrews 7:26). However hopeless you have felt about yourself or someone else, know that nothing is impossible for Jesus Christ. He is able to save all who come to him.

Jesus, you are the Savior of the world, and I believe you are more powerful than my meager mind can comprehend. I trust you can do far more and far better than I can ask. Increase my faith as I pray bolder prayers today.

HOLY CONFESSION

If we confess our sins, He is faithful and just to forgive us our sins and to cleanse us from all unrighteousness.

1 JOHN 1:9 ESV

There is something incredibly beautiful about confession to God or to others. It takes vulnerability and humility. It gives space to the reality of where we are and what we are struggling with while also admitting we want better. It allows another to show up for us in support, love, and accountability when we seek it.

It is not trendy to talk about confession, but it is a necessary part of being known. When we confess our faults and flaws to Christ, he is faithful and just to forgive us. He knows us so well, and he makes space for all of us. He meets our vulnerable risks with the deep compassion of his heart. He covers us with his powerful mercy, and we grow stronger in the light of his love.

Jesus, I know there is no reason to keep anything hidden from you. I don't want pride, fear, or shame to keep me stuck in areas where you have power to break through in my life. I confess to you because I trust you.

DECIDE IN YOUR HEART

You must each decide in your heart how much to give.
And don't give reluctantly or in response to pressure.
"For God loves a person who gives cheerfully."

2 CORINTHIANS 9:7 NLT

There is no right strategy for generosity within our lives.
We love a good system and three-point directive to get
from point A to point B, but Jesus taught more in parables
that underlined the guiding values of our lives than he did
with rigid rules.

If we want to give from a place of authenticity, let's not
look at what our neighbors and friends are doing to match
them; let's decide what is right for us. We should not give
because we are pressured to do so. Instead, we should
search within ourselves to find the amount (or time, talent,
or item) that aligns with us. Whenever we give, whether it
be big or small, let's do it willingly and cheerfully, for that
reflects God.

*Jesus, I love that you are never reluctant in offering your
mercy. You do not begrudgingly help those who ask for it.
You do it willingly and with joy. I want to give in the same
way. Thank you for this shift in my thinking.*

KEEP TRUSTING

Do not throw away this confident trust in the Lord.
Remember the great reward it brings you!

HEBREWS 10:35 NLT

What was it like for you when you first came to know
Jesus? What were those early days filled with after Christ
shined the light of his love on your life? Were you bolder in
faith than you are now? Were you more willing to reach out
in compassion to others?

Whatever the case may be, whatever has changed in your
life, may you keep boldly trusting the Lord for all you need.
Change is inevitable and not a fault. Jesus is not finished
working his mercy through the details of your story. Even
what feels wasted to you is not wasted to him. Press into
the present love of Christ through the Spirit today. He loves
you as much now as he ever has, and he always will.

*Jesus, I keep choosing to trust in you. You are my
confidence. Even when everything else is turned on its
head, you remain constant. Strengthen my heart in your
love and lead me in your grace.*

WHAT JOY

Oh, what joy for those whose disobedience is forgiven,
whose sin is put out of sight!

PSALM 32:1 NLT

Christ has set you free from the talons of sin and death.
He has liberated you from the lies of shame and fear that
sought to control you and keep you small. What will you
do with this freedom? Whatever you do, do not forget the
joy that comes with it.

When you come to Christ, seeking his forgiveness and
help, he covers you with mercy. Psalm 103:2 says he has
removed your sin as far as the east is from the west. There
is no end to the compassion he offers, and he tenderly
cares for you the way a kind and good father cares for his
children. May the joy of his love burst within your heart as
you meditate on how great his goodness is toward you.

*Jesus, thank you for removing my sin from your sight. You
do not hold against me what you have already forgiven.
I'm so grateful. When shame rears its ugly head and tries
to diminish my worth, I will remember what you have
already done and rejoice in the freedom that is mine.*

POWERFUL MESSAGE

The message of the cross is foolishness to those who are perishing, but to us who are being saved it is the power of God.

1 Corinthians 1:18 NKJV

Christ's sacrifice—his humble life, death, and resurrection—is the power of God made manifest in the earth. The message of the cross is that God's love knew no end. It knew no boundary or stopping point. Christ's sacrifice removed any barrier that remained between God and humanity. Through Christ, we come to the Father without blame, blemish, or fear.

Jesus is our Savior, and there is no other like him. As the Son of God, he did not sin. He did, however, live the human experience. He knew hunger, he knew weariness, and he knew the blame of others thrown at him. Still, he chose to come. He chose to extend mercy. He chose to die. When the grave could not keep him, he chose to rise again. What a powerfully humble and beautifully compassionate God!

Jesus, would you give me greater insight into the power of your love that compelled you to go to the cross? I want to know you more in spirit and in truth. Thank you for providing a way of help, salvation, and freedom.

HEART FELLOWSHIP

I have hidden your word in my heart
that I might not sin against you.

PSALM 119:11 NIV

It is not enough to know a person through what they choose to present in curated messages, snapshots, and snippets of their life. Consider how different it is to know a person solely through social media rather than real life. We can have our ideas about who a person may or may not be based on their profile, but we do not see them in the messy moments.

We know people in the nitty-gritty of the mundane and in the lows as much as the highs. We see them in the disappointments and setbacks as much as the victories. It is the same with knowing Christ. We can know about him, or we can truly get to know him in the routines of our days. We have fellowship with his Spirit, and we have his Word to direct us. May we give ourselves to actually knowing him and not just making assumptions about him based on popular moments.

Jesus, I know you experienced hardship and you experienced pain. I want to know you in my life, walk with you, hear your voice, and rely on your present grace. I will hide your Word in my heart and live to know you more.

UNCONTAINABLE JOY

May God, the inspiration and fountain of hope, fill you to overflowing with uncontainable joy and perfect peace as you trust in him. And may the power of the Holy Spirit continually surround your life with his super-abundance until you radiate with hope!

ROMANS 15:13 TPT

As you choose to trust in Christ and his power in your life, may it not simply remain in the space of your conscious thoughts. May God, who is the inspiration and fountain of hope, fill you to overflowing with uncontainable joy. This kind of joy bubbles up from the inside and moves through your body.

May he fill you to bursting with his perfect peace as you trust in him. There is a deep-seated peace for you no matter what is going on in your world. It transcends understanding and calms your fears. May you be continually surrounded by the power of the Holy Spirit in every area of your life until you radiate with hope!

Jesus, I want to radiate with your joy and hope as the light of your life alive in me. I want to know the deep and abiding peace of your presence. Holy Spirit, surround me today and encourage my heart in hope.

BETTER THAN LIFE ITSELF

Your tender mercies mean more to me than life itself.
How I love and praise you, God!

PSALM 63:3 TPT

The mercy of God is powerful. It is enough to burst through the grave and defeat death. The mercy of God is also tender and cares for the most vulnerable among us with compassion. If you have experienced the mercy of God holding you together when you were coming apart at the seams, then you know this tenderness.

May you experience greater measures of his love as you meditate on his goodness today. Look to Christ, the gardener of your faith. He both planted the seed and tends to it. May you find that as you partner with him, you see the fingerprints of his mercy in places you didn't even know to look. He is just that good.

Jesus, your mercies toward me have given me life. They have nourished and restored me. I trust there is even more to come; you will not let up your hand on my life. I love and praise you!

DECEMBER

God is our refuge and strength,
an ever-present help in trouble.

PSALM 46:1 NIV

ANCHOR OF HOPE

We have this hope as an anchor for the soul,
firm and secure.

HEBREWS 6:19 NIV

What is this unshakable hope that the writer of Hebrews is talking about? It is the faithful vow that God made through Christ. It is the promise to fulfill everything he said he would. We have been saved by grace, and the faith we put in Jesus cannot be moved, for he who called us is faithful.

The anchor of hope keeps our souls connected to the faithfulness of God, and he will never fail. He won't abandon his promises or his people. He will follow through on every vow he has made, and he will do it with power and mercy. As we fix our eyes on Jesus today, may our souls know the deep, abiding hope that is ours.

Jesus, thank you for your faithfulness. I do not have to wonder whether you will follow through on your word, for I know you will. You are loyal in love, and you are steadfast in truth. Hallelujah!

OVERFLOWING BLESSINGS

You honor me by anointing my head with oil.
My cup overflows with blessings.

PSALM 23:5 NLT

Psalm 23 starts with David saying, "The Lord is my shepherd; I have all that I need." When we give the Lord leadership of our lives and submit to his guidance and tender care, we have no reason to worry or fear. He is our protector, the keeper of our souls, and our loving leader.

Anointing a person's head with oil is a ritual act of pouring fragrant oil over them, typically signifying a ceremonial blessing. The Lord has blessed us by pouring over us the aromatic oil of the Holy Spirit. He is our covering, our blessing, and the fragrance of God's blessing over our lives. We have overflowing blessings in him.

Jesus, thank you for your Spirit whom you pour so freely over those who love you. You are my shepherd and my guide. I love being known as yours!

BEAUTIFUL SPIRIT

Let your adorning be the hidden person of the heart
with the imperishable beauty of a gentle and quiet
spirit, which in God's sight is very precious.

1 PETER 3:4 ESV

There is nothing wrong with valuing how we display
ourselves in the world. Whether through how we dress, our
hairstyles, or other personal choices, our greatest value
is not in what we present outwardly. Our souls' health
matters so much more. True beauty is in the cultivation of
our hearts with love and peace.

Our bodies age and change, but our souls only grow in
complexity and beauty as they mature in the light of God's
love. Instead of idolizing youth, let's age gracefully in our
bodies, minds, hearts, and souls. Let's tend to the gardens
of our hearts with the help of the Holy Spirit and continue
to heal in his restorative love.

*Jesus, I know you value what is in my heart and you value
the container it is in. May I be whole in your living love in
body, soul, and spirit. May I be full of your perfect peace
as I align with your kingdom values.*

DO YOUR BEST

In all the work you are doing, work the best you can.
Work as if you were doing it for the Lord,
not for people.

COLOSSIANS 3:23 NCV

In this hectic holiday season, it can feel as if all the work we're doing is not enough to get ahead. There are errands to run, parties to attend, work to finish up before year's end, and so much more. Take this as your cue to slow down, do what you can, and simplify the rest. Let go of what you cannot get to. In fact, this may be a good time to reevaluate whether everything you're trying to do is necessary.

Take some time with the Lord today and ask for his perspective over your schedule. What are the most important things to focus on? What can you let go of? When you have a better idea of what you have to do today, work as if you are partnering with Jesus himself. Do your best and let go of the rest.

Jesus, I want to use my time wisely and expend my energy with vision. Help me to prioritize well. No matter what I do, I do it for you.

BE CONSISTENT

Each one of you should continue to live the way God
has given you to live—the way you were when God
called you.

1 Corinthians 7:17 ncv

When we align our lives with Christ, it does not mean we
have to give up everything we've worked for in life. In
fact, Paul's admonition to the believers at Corinth was to
continue to live the way they were when God called them.
If you have a business, manage that business for Christ. If
you are a lawyer, let the transformative power of Christ's
love within you empower you to work to bring justice.

You do not have to have a church ministry to make a
difference in the kingdom. You do not have to shift your
entire life in order to please God. Unless you have clarity
about shifting to something else, stay the course and in all
you do, do it as unto the Lord. There is beauty in growing
where you are already planted.

*Jesus, thank you for the realization that my gifts,
strengths, and assets can be used to serve you right where
I am. I don't have to go to specialized ministry schools or
far-off lands to serve you. I will follow you right here.*

EVERYTHING EVERYWHERE

The earth is the LORD's, and everything in it.
The world and all its people belong to him.

PSALM 24:1 NLT

How different would our lives look if we truly lived by the belief that everything in the earth is the Lord's? Would we be more open-hearted to those who look different from us? Would we be more willing to see the beauty in diversity rather than the threat of it?

Everything, everywhere, as the psalmist says, is the Lord's. All the people of the world belong to him: not just you, not just me. His land is not only where our feet have tread. His people are not only those we are drawn to naturally. There is a big world out there, full of various expressions of God's image, and we can learn to delight in them. May our mindsets shift from being wary of differences to seeing the wonder in them.

Jesus, I'm humbled by your love, and I'm reminded of how much greater you are when I see the vastness of the world. I'm glad that you're not limited by anything, and that includes my ideas of how you move. You are as vast and glorious as the world around me and beyond.

UNSWERVING HOPE

Let us hold unswervingly to the hope we profess,
for he who promised is faithful.

HEBREWS 10:23 NIV

The fulfillment of our hopes does not rely on us. Jesus is
the source of our hope. He is the sustainer of it, and he will
follow through on every promise he made. He is absolutely
unchanging in love, unmoved by the threats of the world,
and undiminished by our struggles. What a beautiful and
liberating truth that is!

Our confidence is in Christ. It is in his mercy. It is in his
work on the cross, his resurrection from death, and his
coming return. He has given us the Holy Spirit as a seal to
his promise. We know Christ more fully through fellowship
with the Spirit. Wherever we are, whatever we're facing,
our hope is sure, and the promises of God are guaranteed.

*Jesus, my hope is in you and not in myself. Help me not
get distracted by my limitations, and may I trust in you
more and more. Ground me in the reality of your love and
set me free from the anxiety of fear. I trust you.*

MY COURAGE

Lord, where do I put my hope?
My only hope is in you.

PSALM 39:7 NLT

David prefaces this statement of hope with the realization that what we often work for in life does not compare to God and his goodness. Psalm 39:5-6 says, "My entire lifetime is just a moment to you; at best, each of us is but a breath. We are merely moving shadows, and all our busy rushing ends in nothing. We heap up wealth, not knowing who will spend it."

May we come to the same conclusion as David did as we consider the scope of our lives. Our only, our greatest, and our truest hope is in Christ. We have a firm anchor of hope in him. He is not swayed by the opinions of this world. He is steadfast and true, and he will never let us down. He is better than we are and more loyal to his word than we are to our own. He is good, he is faithful, and he is our unswerving hope.

Jesus, there is no one else like you. My life is but a breath in the great scope of humanity, yet you love me. You care for me. You are with me! May every breath I breathe today be laced with the gratitude overflowing from my heart.

TRUE SATISFACTION

You open your hand;
you satisfy the desire of every living thing.

PSALM 145:16 ESV

David declares earlier in this beautiful and uplifting psalm that he will meditate on the glorious splendor of God's majesty and on his wondrous works. Let's take David's lead today as we consider the wondrous works of God. More specifically, let's meditate on the glorious splendor of his majesty through the life of Christ.

Jesus is the source of our true satisfaction. He has resources to strengthen us with his grace, to uphold us in his mercy, and to satisfy us with his peace. He is better to us than we are to one another. He is full of wisdom to guide us into the ways of his everlasting kingdom. We have all we need in his resurrection power, and he will never leave us to fight our battles alone.

Jesus, thank you for your presence with me. On my hardest days, I will remember what you have said, what you have done, and how you have faithfully followed through on your Word. I will not abandon hope, for my soul knows true satisfaction in the purity of your love.

CLOTHED IN LOVE

Above all, clothe yourselves with love,
which binds us all together in perfect harmony.

COLOSSIANS 3:14 NLT

Love binds together all the values of God's kingdom. True love is not simply a feeling or a choice. It is the power of God. It is more than we can imagine, stronger than we can rightly grasp, and yet it is the path Christ calls us to.

When Christ declared that the whole of the law could be summed up in the golden rule to love others as we love ourselves (or to prefer them over our own biases), he was inviting us into a greater understanding of what love covers. Surely to uphold justice is loving, to share our resources is loving, and to stand on truth is loving. May we not limit ourselves in the understanding of God's love, for it is expansive and ever transforming our hearts, minds, and lives in the greater reality of God's kingdom.

Jesus, I don't want to limit your love. I don't want a stale and small definition of what your love looks like, either. I choose to clothe myself in your kindness, mercy, and strength. I invite you to expand my understanding as I follow and choose your ways over my own.

HEART'S DESIRE

My God, I want to do what you want.
Your teachings are in my heart.

PSALM 40:8 NCV

Have you ever been overcome by the feeling David describes in this verse? *My God, I want to do what you want.* When we meditate on the Word of God, when we seek to know Jesus more through the written accounts of his life and words, our hearts are almost sure to grow in this desire.

Whatever our hearts' desires, there is wisdom in letting the pursuit of God drive us to know him more. The more we meditate on his Word, the more we get to know what he is like. The more we fellowship with him in his Spirit, the deeper our love for him grows. May he be the greatest desire of our hearts; may following his loving lead be the joy of our lives.

Jesus, I don't want to follow in the ways of those who end up in foolishness and despair. All the wealth in the world is meaningless without your love active in my life. I don't want to live simply for myself and my desires. I want to satisfy you. Lead me, Lord.

MINDFUL UNDERSTANDING

Don't act thoughtlessly,
but understand what the Lord wants you to do.

EPHESIANS 5:17 NLT

Living with wisdom does not follow a prescriptive path. It will look different from person to person, and the value systems of God's kingdom will motivate each one in their own way. The fruit of the Spirit is evident in all those who submit their hearts, lives, and choices to Christ. Thoughtful living leads us in purpose and passion.

Do you understand what the Lord wants you to do? It doesn't have to be a specific job or calling, but those can be great gifts of vision for us. What is more important than what we do is how we do it. Be mindful about your choices and let them be full of the fruit of the Spirit who lives within you.

Jesus, thank you for wisdom that leads me to choose mindfully how I will live. I don't want to get so swept up into the busyness of my life that I miss the important things. As I look to you today, may your Spirit's presence direct and redirect me in wisdom and peace.

STRENGTH AND PEACE

The LORD gives his people strength.
The LORD blesses them with peace.

PSALM 29:11 NLT

When you find yourself weary or weak, know this: the Lord can give you strength. When your heart is restless with the anxiety of unknowns and the overwhelming sorrow of injustice in the world, may you find that Christ blesses you with peace.

There is grace enough to keep hanging on in this moment. Loving kindness surrounds us to strengthen our hearts in hope of Christ's kingdom. There is more than what meets the eye. There is more: love that expands, hope that resurrects joy, and faith that holds onto the faithfulness of Christ. May you find all you need in the living presence of God's Spirit with you today.

Jesus, give me your strength and fill me with your peace. I need you more than I can express. My heart, my hope, and my very life depend on you. I rely on your presence to strengthen and uphold me. I rely on you, Jesus.

MINISTRY OF RECONCILIATION

God has made all things new, and reconciled us to himself, and given us the ministry of reconciling others to God.

2 CORINTHIANS 5:18 TPT

Christ has purified us in the mercy of his sacrifice. What a powerful truth! Verse 17 of this chapter states, if anyone is enfolded into Christ, he has become an entirely new person. Everything is fresh and new. It is from this place, as a purified people, that we have been reconciled to God. It is also from this place that we have been given the ministry of reconciliation.

When was the last time you shared your experience of faith and fellowship with God with another? Have you shared a testimony of his goodness or encouraged someone in his love? Have you shared how merciful, strong, and faithful he is? Have you been clear that the invitation to know God is an open one for all? These are just a few questions to spur your prayer life and consider how you can participate in the reconciliation ministry of Christ in your life.

Jesus, thank you for your purifying love. I am a new creation in you and fully alive in your mercy. Continue to refine my heart in the truth of who you are and draw others to you through the living sacrifice of my life.

FRAGRANT OFFERING

Let my prayer be as the evening sacrifice
that burns like fragrant incense,
rising as my offering to you
as I lift up my hands in surrendered worship!

PSALM 141:2 TPT

Wherever this finds you today, no matter the greatness of your joy or the depth of your despair, may you take the opportunity to lift your prayer to God as an offering to him. Don't withhold your attention or your experience. He is neither impressed by you nor surprised by you. Your Father knows you through and through.

Let your prayer rise with surrendered worship to the one who knows you well. David penned these words with an urgent need for God's help. If you are desperate for God's help, press into the place of prayer. Perhaps read all the way through today's psalm. Turn your heart to the Lord. He is near.

Jesus, thank you for your present help in times of trouble. I offer you my prayers in the morning and the evening. Every time I turn my attention to you, let it be like fragrant incense rising to you.

HOLY BELONGING

Accept one another, then, just as Christ accepted you,
in order to bring praise to God.

ROMANS 15:7 NIV

All who call on the name of the Lord are answered. All who
belong to the kingdom of Christ belong to him. Instead
of drawing lines of division based on our differences, let's
accept one another in lovingkindness just as Christ has
accepted each of us.

It is holy to hold space for each other. It is godly to look
for the things that unite us rather than divide us. Christ's
grace is so much larger than we can imagine, and there
is room for all of us. Let's lay down the need to compete
and instead search for ways we can build each other up
and encourage one another. In unity, we will find greater
strength.

*Jesus, thank you for your acceptance of each person who
submits her heart to you. I don't want to get caught up in
the divisions that are so clear to see. I want to promote
your peace, live with your love as my motivation, and
know the strength of being part of your family.*

GREATER THAN TEMPTATION

The temptations in your life are no different from what others experience. And God is faithful. He will not allow the temptation to be more than you can stand. When you are tempted, he will show you a way out so that you can endure.

1 CORINTHIANS 10:13 NLT

When we are caught up in our isolated experiences, we can feel alone in what we are going through. Though the details of our situations and problems may vary, our felt response is shared. Whatever we are going through, someone else has already walked through it. Whatever hardship we face has already been faced, and is being faced, by others.

This is not meant to make you feel small! It's meant to connect you. The human experience is full of temptations to give into fear or scarcity, to shut others out instead of inviting them in, and so much more. God is faithful in our temptations and provides us a way out. His love gives us courage to reach out, and it gives us strength to persevere.

Jesus, thank you for the grace of your presence and the grace of fellowship with others. I lean into you for all I need, and I press on in perseverance to keep following your ways.

JOY IS ON ITS WAY

Weeping may last through the night,
but joy comes with the morning.

PSALM 30:5 NLT

We cannot avoid pain in our lives. It is part of living, and no one gets out of it. Rather than be discouraged by this fact, may we take heart in the promises of Christ. Even though weeping lasts for a dark season, joy will surely come in the light of the rising sun over our lives. The sun is constantly shining even when we are in the dark.

Just as the earth turns and morning comes again, so will our lives turn, and the joyful relief of a new day will dawn upon us. This is a great hope! If you are grieving, you don't have to pretend it is morning; just know that it will come again. Hope will rise on the wings of the dawn, and you will be refreshed in the delight of a new day. In that light, you will see clearly what you cannot now. Hold on.

Jesus, thank you for the promise of fresh joy coming. Even as I weep, I know it won't last forever. I put my hope in you.

GIFTED TO SERVE

God has given each of you a gift from his great variety of spiritual gifts. Use them well to serve one another.

1 PETER 4:10 NLT

Every gift and talent we have is not simply for our own use. What meaning is there in life without connection to others? In the same way that we love those close to us and we use our gifts to benefit them, let's also use our gifts for the greater good of our communities.

We use our gifts well when we learn to serve one another in love. Everything has a purpose in God's kingdom. There are no insignificant acts of love in the eyes of God. It all matters. Mercy makes a difference even if no one else ever acknowledges or recognizes it. God keeps record, and he will reward our faith. How can you use your strengths to serve someone in love today?

Jesus, you were known as the servant of all. I know laid-down love is the way of the cross, and it's the way of your kingdom. Show me how and whom I can serve today with kindness and intention.

GLORY OF GOD

Not to us, LORD,
not to us but to your name be the glory,
because of your love and faithfulness.

PSALM 115:1 NIV

When we live with humility in our hearts, we understand that it does not matter what kind of glory or notoriety we get in this life. Every accolade loses its luster eventually. What is achieved does not satisfy for long. Let's join with the psalmist even in our greatest victories and say: "Not to us, Lord...but to your name be the glory."

The Lord is full of love and faithfulness forever. When we align our lives with the kingdom of Christ, we offer him the glory over and over again. Whatever is our gain in this life is to God's glory. Whatever brings us to our knees is also an opportunity for God to receive glory. His grace is made perfect in our weakness. Whatever we face today, whatever triumphs or defeats, let it all be to the glory of God.

Jesus, I don't want to overly value the praise of others. I also don't want to underplay the importance of your mercy's work in my life. I give you glory, and I ask for your perspective to transform my understanding and inform my praise.

HE WILL STILL DO IT

He delivered us from such a deadly peril, and he will
deliver us. On him we have set our hope that he will
deliver us again.

2 CORINTHIANS 1:10 ESV

God has delivered his people, and he will deliver them.
We see this happen throughout the Old Testament. Israel
needed help over and over throughout their history instead
of only once. They needed God daily, and so do we.

Through Christ, we have intimate fellowship with the Father
through the Spirit. We do not have to wait for the day
when we stand face-to-face with him to have a relationship
with God. We have it now. Let's not waste another moment
thinking that we are alone in our trials. We are never alone.
Christ has delivered us, and he will continue to deliver us.
What a hopeful reality there is in him.

*Jesus, I don't want to conjure faith out of thin air. I want
to know the overwhelming peace of your presence
that builds up my faith in you. I believe that just as you
have come through before, you will continue to do in
faithfulness. I trust you.*

WORK IT OUT

The LORD will work out his plans for my life—
for your faithful love, O LORD, endures forever.
Don't abandon me, for you made me.

PSALM 138:8 NLT

The faithful love of God lasts forever. From the dawning of the universe, when God spoke and there was light, to the end of this age when Christ returns to the earth, the faithful love of God continues. It is not measured by human logic, and it cannot be contained by us. It is so much larger, so much purer, and so much more powerful than we can comprehend.

The plans of the Lord will be worked out in our lives as we trust him. They may not look how we expect, but they will speak of his love for us. His plans for us are so much better than our own. We don't even know how to ask for what he wants for us, but he faithfully reveals his kindness to us anyway. What a beautiful hope. What a beautiful God!

Jesus, I believe that you will work out your plans for my life in better ways than I can imagine. I find that the more I know you, the less it takes to satisfy my ambitions. You are better than life itself.

A FAITHFUL LIFE

I have fought the good fight,
I have finished the race,
I have kept the faith.

2 TIMOTHY 4:7 NCV

What would it take for you to echo the words of Paul at the end of your life? What are the driving values of your life? What do you want to be known for? How does that show up in your day-to-day lifestyle? Does the way you spend your time reflect where you want to be at the end of your life?

Whatever your goals, may you know the all-surpassing goodness of knowing God. May you know the grace and strength of his presence empowering you to persevere when you'd rather give up. May you know the incomparable peace of being cared for by the King of kings. His love is stronger than death. His mercy is greater than your failures. May Christ's faithfulness to you be fodder for praise, and may you continually surrender your life to his love.

Jesus, when my days are over and my life draws to a close, I want to be known as one who lived with love as my greatest goal and my greatest achievement. May my relationships reflect the mercy of your heart. I live for you.

ALL IN LOVE

Let all that you do
be done in love.

1 CORINTHIANS 16:14 NRSV

In all we do, in staying alert to God's truth and holding firmly to our faith in him, may we be mighty and full of courage. Let kindness and love be the motivation behind everything we do. Is that not the call of Christ? We cannot overstate the importance of love in our lives. We cannot underestimate the power of it.

If you find yourself surrounded by loved ones this Christmas, don't forget the most important thing that brings you together. God's love toward us in sending his Son gives us a glimpse into the kind of loyal love we can lavish on each other. Whatever you do this holiday, do it in love.

Jesus, I remember how you came to earth, wrapped in flesh and bones as a baby, and how you lived your life growing in the knowledge of the Lord. In the pinnacle of your life and ministry, you continued to remind those who followed you of the importance of God's love. You are doing it still; I won't devalue the power of it.

WONDERFUL COUNSELOR

"A child has been born to us; God has given a son to us. He will be responsible for leading the people. His name will be Wonderful Counselor, Powerful God, Father Who Lives Forever, Prince of Peace."

ISAIAH 9:6 NCV

The prophet Isaiah foretold the birth of Christ in this familiar passage of Scripture. If you have gone to church during Advent, you have probably heard this passage spoken or sung. The prophecy gave a glimpse into what we know was the life of Christ, the Messiah.

As you meditate on the first Christmas when Jesus was born, may you grasp a little bit more of the marvelous mystery of Christ with us. Emmanuel. God with us. Jesus is the Prince of our Peace. He is our Wonderful Counselor. He is Powerful God as seen through his resurrection. He is the Father who lives forever, for the Spirit, Son, and Father are one. Offer him the praise that rises within you. Honor him with your life today and every day.

Jesus, I don't want to only remember you on Christmas and Easter. I want to know the power of your life within mine every day of the year. Thank you for coming to earth, for experiencing humanity, and for showing us the way to the Father. I worship you!

A GOOD LIFE

Be joyful. Grow to maturity.
Encourage each other.
Live in harmony and peace.
Then the God of love and peace will be with you.

2 CORINTHIANS 13:11 NLT

This verse is a benediction from Paul. It is a blessing and an encouragement at the closing of his second letter to the believers in Corinth. After a day of celebration yesterday, you may find yourself just wanting to rest and recuperate today. Enjoy this time rather than be let down by it.

Be joyful for whatever is yours. Continue to grow to maturity; that might look like giving yourself space to clean, rest, or spend time with your loved ones. Encourage each other. Don't give up speaking words of life to those around you. Live in harmony and peace. Don't let little squabbles keep you from loving each other. *Then the God of love and peace will be with you.* May you know his presence in your midst today.

Jesus, thank you for your presence and your goodness. Where I might feel discouraged today, I ask for your perspective to shift my own.

EVERY LONGING

O Lord, all my longing is known to you;
my sighing is not hidden from you.

Psalm 38:9 NRSV

Weary heart, may you be encouraged by knowing God sees you today. He knows every longing lurking in your soul. He knows the desires you have hidden there. He knows your struggle, and he is with you in it. He has not left you. He will never abandon you. His loyal love reaches toward you with the affection of his embrace even now.

For those who are not weary but who rub shoulders with the burdened, may you bear witness to those who are struggling without trying to fix them. May you continue to surround them with support and love. May you know that, even in this, you are reflecting the merciful heart of God. Partner with his heart, for he won't fail.

Jesus, disappointment is no match for your love. Cover us with your mercy and lift our heavy burdens with the relief of your presence. Thank you.

UNASHAMED

Make every effort to give yourself to God as the kind of person he will approve. Be a worker who is not ashamed and who uses the true teaching in the right way.

2 TIMOTHY 2:15 NCV

When we live our lives in submission to Christ and his love, letting his leadership inform our decisions, there is no reason to be ashamed. When we are aligned in the values of God's kingdom more than we are concerned with what others think of us, we are on the right path of his love. Don't get tripped up by the opinions of those who do not matter. Show them love, yes, but don't give them power to speak into your life when they have no real say. Give yourself to God. Live with kindness, mercy, and integrity, and don't worry about what others think. You get to decide how you will live, and you get to do it unashamedly.

Jesus, I'm so grateful for your liberating love. I get to live for your kingdom come without shame or blame. When others misunderstand my motives, I know you do not. I am not ashamed of the gospel of your peace, and I will continue to follow your path of laid-down love.

KINGDOM OF TRUTH

Your kingdom is built on what is right and fair.
Love and truth are in all you do.

PSALM 89:14 NCV

God cannot lie. He does not manipulate or control us. He is full of justice. He is full of truth. He sees everything clearly, and he cannot be tricked. *The kingdom of God is built on what is right and fair.* There is no hidden shadow in Christ.

Though we try to figure out what is right, fair, and true, our understanding is only in part. We don't see the end from the beginning as God does. Humility is necessary to walk in the light of his truth. It admits that there is always more to learn, more to know, and more ways to grow. The kingdom of Christ is unmovable, and there is love and truth in everything he does. Instead of following the path that others are forging, let's choose to follow Christ. His ways are better.

Jesus, I know the fruit of your truth is in the world. Instead of rigid rules, you gave us values to follow. You told us that if we truly love others, we are aligned in your ways. I follow you, for you are the truth.

SAME GOD

God works in different ways,
but it is the same God who does the work in all of us.

1 CORINTHIANS 12:6 NLT

Let's not get too caught up in how God works in each of our lives. God is always doing something new. He is not a cookie-cutter God. He delights in difference and diversity. He is creative. Instead of looking for duplicates, let's look past the surface.

God said in 1 Samuel 16:7 that he doesn't see things the way we see them. People judge by outward appearance, but the Lord looks at the heart. Instead of judging someone based on the way they do things, look instead for the fruit of the things they do. In Matthew 7:20, Jesus encouraged his followers to do just that: "Just as you can identify a tree by its fruit, so you can identify people by their actions." Let's take it straight from the source and rely on his wisdom to inform our lives.

Jesus, I trust that your ways are better than my own. It's not my job to judge others; I am to love them. Your wisdom says the fruit of a surrendered life will bear your kingdom's fruit. I trust your work in my own life and in others' lives.

FOREVER WATCHED OVER

The LORD will watch over your coming and going
both now and forevermore.

PSALM 121:8 NIV

As this year draws to an end and you reflect on it, may
you do so with the lens of God's grace. May you see where
Christ's mercy met you, sustained you, and liberated you.
May you rejoice in the ways that his victory is clear. May
you give thanks for the areas where perseverance led to
growth and maturity.

As you look ahead to next year, perhaps with hopeful
expectation, may the confidence of God go with you into
the unknown. He has not left you yet, and he won't now.
May you have vision and consistency to grow even more
in grace this coming year. Above all else, may you know
the love that surpasses knowledge and be filled to all the
fullness of God (Ephesians 3:19).

*Jesus, you have watched over my comings and my goings,
and I trust you will continue to do so. Your loyal love builds
me up and keeps me growing. I trust you, I love you, and
I delight in you. Thank you, Jesus, for all you've done and
for all you will do!*